# The Tale Spinner

## Folktales, Themes, and Activities

Linda K. Garrity

Illustrated by Emilia Markovich

**fulcrum resources**

**Golden, Colorado**

For Bonnie Heather and Meghan Katie, my best audience

**Library of Congress Cataloging-in-Publication Data**
Garrity, Linda K.
      The tale spinner : folktales, themes, and activities / by Linda K. Garrity ; illustrated by Emilia Markovich.
          p.       cm.
      Includes bibliographical references and indexes.
      ISBN 1-55591-970-7
      1. Tales—Study and teaching (Elementary)   2. Multiculturalism—Study and teaching (Elementary)   3. Folklore and children.   I. Title
      GR45.G37 1999
      372.8—dc21                                                           98–32134
                                                                                    CIP

*Text design by Dovetail Publishing Services*
*Cover design by Alyssa Pumphrey*

Printed in the United States of America
10   9   8   7   6   5   4   3   2   1

Fulcrum Publishing
350 Indiana Street, Suite 350
Golden, Colorado 80401-5093
(800) 992-2908 • (303) 277-1624
website: www.fulcrum-resources.com
e-mail: fulcrum@fulcrum-resources.com

# Table of Contents

## Chapter 1
## Beware of Strangers
*(African-American, Chinese, and German folktales)*

## Chapter 2
## Turnabout Is Fair Play
*(African, Burmese, Mexican, and African-American folktales)*

# Chapter 3
# Don't Believe Everything You Hear
*(African, Belgian, German, Indian, and Russian folktales)*

# Chapter 4
# Origin of Thunder
*(African, Australian, and Native American folktales)*

# Chapter 5
# Origin of Fire

*(Eskimo, Native American, and Polynesian folktales)*

# Chapter 6
# Spinning Tales

*(Cornish and English folktale books, plus German and Irish folktales)*

# Chapter 7
# Cooperation Pays

*(German, Irish, Puerto Rican, Russian, and Slovenian folktales)*

# Chapter 8
# Never Give Up (The Cinderella Theme)

*(African, Appalachian American, Brazilian, Irish, Italian, Korean, Native American, Norwegian, and Vietnamese folktales)*

# The Origin of Folklore

For centuries folktales were passed on orally. Older generations told younger generations in a continuous pattern, though this only partially explains the spread of the stories. Sailors, who have navigated the waters of the world from the dawn of time, have always retold tales wherever they have landed. Folklorists (scholars who study folktales) feel that stories that traveled by water were altered the least, according to Zena Sutherland (*Children and Books*. Glenview, Ill. Scott, Foresman, 1981). Stories also traveled by land. Entertainers, such as minstrels, acrobats, jugglers, and actors, used folktales as part of their performances. Religious figures (priests and monks), adventurers, and wanderers often told stories in exchange for something to eat and a place to sleep. People on the move, either of their own accord or to escape hostilities, kept their stories in their hearts and souls and passed them on to others in new lands. Much folklore was spread by people taken into slavery as nursemaids, who told stories from their native culture to entertain their captors' children.

As folklore traveled, it changed to match the language, values, and settings of the new environments. Sometimes stories from new cultures were combined with those of existing cultures to produce unique folktales. Stories continue to change until they are written down.

The explanation of the movement of folklore from one geographic area to another does not completely satisfy many folklorists. They feel that because feelings of greed, jealousy, love, devotion, and so on are found in all groups of people, it is entirely possible for similar stories to spring up among vastly different peoples throughout the world at varying times in history. They point especially to cultures that have some folktales similar to those found in distant cultures, such as those in the Americas that had very little exchange with Europe or Asia previous to the 1500s.

There are no definitive answers as to the origin of each of the folktales in this book. Some of the themes have only a few variants, while others, like those in the "Never Give Up" theme, have hundreds. It is interesting to speculate on the origin of the stories, as well as to compare and contrast different cultures' folk literature. Awareness and respect for cultural similarities and differences is an integral part of the study of folk literature.

# How to Use This Book

eveloping a greater awareness of and respect for our multicultural society has become an important objective in many school districts across the country and there is no more exciting vehicle to use than the folklore of various cultures. In this book they are explored as variants or similar stories around a theme or motif. The similarities of all people can be seen in the uncanny resemblance of various folktales; yet, the cultural differences (as shown by unique settings, animals, and speech) are just as apparent. This is the essence of cultural diversity: all alike in so many ways and yet all unique.

The eight folktale units can be used with modification for second through fifth grade. The first theme, "Beware of Strangers," is especially effective with primary children, who are so frequently cautioned about strangers. The final theme of the book, "Never Give Up," is appropriate for older children in view of the stimulating discussions on stereotypes in folklore and comparing and contrasting larger numbers of variants. The folktales and activities are highly appealing and easily adaptable to a wide age range.

Before teaching a selected unit, study the Brief Glossary on page xiii to familiarize yourself and your students with the specialized terms used to describe folktales.

In each unit you can help children compare and contrast the features of these similar multicultural folktales by using Venn diagrams on the blackboard or overhead to record similar and different features. Create one set of overlapping circles for the comparison of characters, a different one for plot, ending, setting, and so forth. This builds higher-level thinking skills and leads children to discover that while the characters, settings, and details vary, the theme of each variant within a unit is the same.

Many tales that are difficult to obtain have been reprinted or, if written in antiquated or narrative language, have been rewritten and included in the book. All the units except the last one can be completed in a week. Beginning with chapter 2, each unit contains a geographic map page that gives teachers an opportunity to integrate geography into the study of literature in a meaningful way. Activity pages incorporate science, reading, writing, drama, art, and research skills into creative projects.

Many related folktales are readily available in school libraries and are listed in each theme's annotated bibliography. The varied and beautiful art in many of these books is a treasure to be shared with children. The following list of books provides additional general and historic information on fairy tales and folktales and how to use them effectively in the classroom:

Bettelheim, Bruno. *The Uses of Enchantment: The Meaning and Importance of Fairy Tales.* New York: Knopf, 1976.

Huck, Charlotte S. *Children's Literature in the Elementary School.* New York: Holt, Rinehart & Winston, 1976.

Sutherland, Zena, Dianne L. Monson, and May Hill Arbuthnot. *Children and Books.* Chicago: Scott, Foresman, 1981.

Tatar, Maria. *The Hard Facts of the Grimms' Fairy Tales.* Princeton, N.J.: Princeton University Press, 1987.

Zipes, Jack. *The Brothers Grimm: From Enchanted Forests to the Modern World.* New York: Routledge, 1988.

# Brief Glossary

These are the meanings for these terms as used in this book. Share these definitions with your class; many of the terms are used on the reproducible activity pages.

**Fairy tale:** usually a longer folktale with elements of magic and sometimes romance. "Cinderella" and "The Princess and the Sea Serpent" are considered fairy tales, while "Kho and the Tiger" and "Brer Possum and Brer Snake" are considered folktales. All fairytales are folktales unless they were written by an identifiable author.

**Folklore:** an umbrella term referring to traditional customs, tales, jokes, rhymes, and songs of the common people. Fairytales and folktales are both folklore.

**Folktale:** an imaginary story originally handed down orally by a group of people or a culture. Not all folktales are fairytales.

**Variant:** a different cultural presentation of a similar folktale; for example, all the folktales in the theme "Cooperation Pays" are variants of the same tale.

**Version:** a different retelling and illustration of essentially the same culture's folktale; for example, Michael Hague, Susan Jeffers, and Diane Goode all wrote and illustrated different versions of "Cinderella."

# Acknowledgments

very effort has been made to secure permission for copyrighted material in this volume. Any errors that may have occurred are inadvertent. Stories not listed are assumed to be in the public domain.

### Chapter 2

"Simba the Lion and the Clever Trap" is an original retelling based on "The Trap" from *When the Stones Were Soft* by Eleanor B. Heady, Funk & Wagnalls, 1968; included with permission from Harold Heady.

"Brer Possum and Brer Snake" is reprinted from *The Days When the Animals Talked;* copyright 1977, by William J. Faulkner; copyright 1993, by the Estate of William J. Faulkner. Reprinted by permission of Marie Brown Associates.

"Kho and the Tiger" is an original retelling based on "Master Kho and the Tiger" from *Burmese and Thai Fairy Tales* by Eleanor Brockett, Follett Publishing Company, 1965.

"Señor Coyote and the Tricked Trickster" is reprinted from *Trickster Tales;* copyright 1966, by I. G. Edmonds, J. B. Lippincott Company; included with permission of HarperCollins Publishers.

### Chapter 3

"Who Can You Believe?" is an original retelling based on "Talk" from *Favorite Stories Old & New* by Sidonie Matsner Gruenberg, Doubleday & Company, 1955, *Best-Loved Folk-Tales of the World* by Joanna Cole, Anchor Books, Doubleday & Company, 1982, and *Too Much Talk* by Angela Shelf Medearis, Candlewick Press, 1995.

"Mr. Louse and Mrs. Louse," "The Day the Sky Fell," and "The Cock and the Hen" is from *I Saw a Rocket Walk a Mile;* copyright 1965, by Carl Withers. Reprinted by permission of Henry Holt and Company.

"The Hare and the Rumor" is reprinted from *Fabulous Fables* by Linda K. Garrity, Good Year Books, 1991; reprinted with permission from Scott Foresman, Addison Wesley.

### Chapter 4

"Superman vs. the Forest Giant" is an original retelling based on "The Tale of the Superman" from *African Myths and Legends* by Kathleen Arnott, Henry Z. Walck, Inc., 1962.

"Thunder and Fire" is an original retelling based on "The Rescue of Fire" from *Down the Lonely Mountain* by Jane Louise Curry, Harcourt Brace & World, Inc., 1965; included with permission from Jane Louise Curry.

"The Lodge of the Bear" is reprinted from *Tonweya and the Eagles and Other Lakota Indian Tales* by Rosebud Yellow Robe, The Dial Press, 1979; included with permission from Penguin Books USA.

"Why the Thunder Man Hurls Thunderbolts" is an original retelling loosely based on brief passages from Louis A. Allen's *Time Before Morning: Art and Myth of the Australian Aborigines,* Thomas Crowell Company, 1975; and *Records of the American-Australian Scientific Expedition to Arnhem Land* by Charles P. Mountford, Melbourne University Press, 1956.

### *Chapter 5*

"How the People Got Fire" is reprinted from *How the People Sang the Mountains Up* by Maria Leach. Copyright 1967 by Maria Leach. Used by permission of Viking Penguin, a division of Penguin Books USA Inc.

"How Fire and Water Came to the Far North" is an original retelling of "Magic in the Carved Chest" from *The Rescue of the Sun* by Edythe W. Newell, Albert Whitman & Company, 1970.

### *Chapter 6*

"Eileen and the Three Hags" is an original retelling of "The Widow's Daughter" from *Hiberian Nights* by Seamus MacManus, The Macmillan Company, New York, 1963; included with permission from the Estate of Seamus MacManus.

### *Chapter 7*

"Jack and the Traveling Animals" is an original retelling based on a story with the same title in *Celtic Folk and Fairy Tales* by Joseph Jacobs, G. P. Putnams's Sons, 1923; included with permission from Dover Publications.

"The Traveling Musicians" is an original retelling based on "The Animal Musicians" from *The Three Wishes* by Ricardo E. Alegria, Harcourt, Brace & World, 1969; included with permission from Ricardo E. Alegria.

"The Ox and His Animal Friends" is an original retelling based on "The Animals in Winter" from *Tales from Central Russia*, Kestrel Books, 1976.

"The Bull and His Animal Friends" is an original retelling based on "Five Musicians" from *The Golden Bird: Folktales from Slovenia*, World Publishing, 1969.

### Chapter 8

# Chapter 1

# Beware of Strangers

## Introduction

This multicultural literature unit on the theme of "Beware of Strangers" is ideal for primary-aged children because they are at the age where they receive much adult advice on this important safety issue.

Fortunately, many beautifully illustrated, award-winning variants of this theme are readily available to share with youngsters. Begin with a variant of the Brothers Grimms' *Little Red Riding Hood*. Then add the Caldecott Award winner *Lon Po Po* from China. The third picture-book variant to share is Patricia McKissack's delightful African-American folktale *Flossie and the Fox*. James Marshall's hilarious version and the clever parodies listed in the annotated bibliography on pages 10–12 should also be included if possible. These resources will provide exciting story sharing sessions and interesting discussions that compare and contrast the different books and illustrative styles.

### Comprehension

The appealing follow-up activities included can be used throughout the unit. After reading the first three books, use the comprehension reproducible page "Baskets." Brainstorm the possibilities for the last basket with the children. Without defined parameters, the last basket can turn out more creatively than you imagined!

### Mapping

The "Map to Grandmother's House" is a story map that can be used as a simple activity or it can be used as a higher-level thinking project by instructing children to add both the wolf's path and the woodcutter's. Allow them to decide what type of line or footprints and colors to use. Labeling important points along each character's path requires thinking and writing skills. A discussion of setting fits in well here. What type of house does Grandmother live in? What kinds of trees and flowers grow there? What would the map look like if Grandmother lived in the city or the jungle? Some children may choose to create a map with a different setting.

## Art

The two pop-up activities are great fun for children to make. The "Pop-Up Wolf" directions and assembly are easier than the "Little Red" pop-up.

## Writing

Use writing "Wolf's Letter" to generate a discussion of point of view in literature. The original tale is from Little Red Riding Hood's point of view, but, with discussion, children can understand how changing the point of view drastically alters the content of the story. Discuss how the story would change if told from the woodcutter's point of view or Grandmother's.

## Drama

A creative drama activity can evolve from the discussion of point of view in literature. For instance, a television news anchor could report this story on the evening news, with a roving reporter interviewing each of the characters for their point of view.

# Baskets

*Directions:* Baskets played an important part in the folktales you have heard. Use crayons or markers to draw what was in each basket. Then draw what you would take to a sick grandmother.

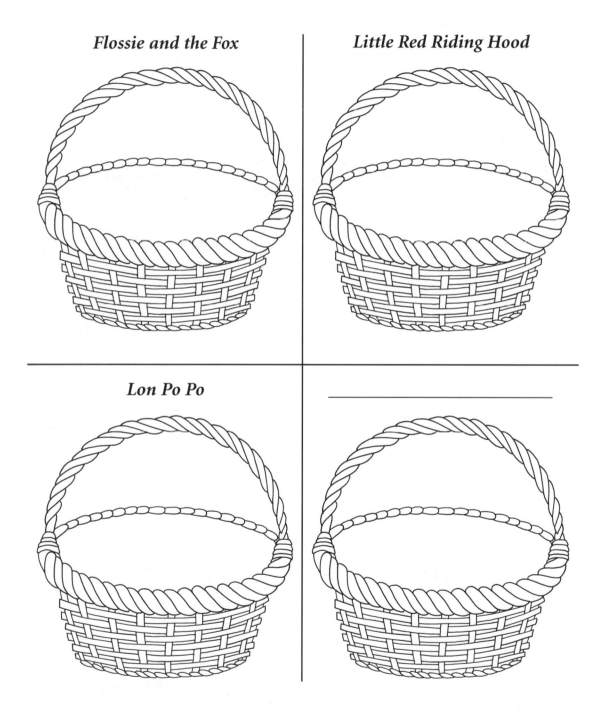

**Flossie and the Fox**

**Little Red Riding Hood**

**Lon Po Po**

_____

# Map to Grandmother's House

*Directions:* Finish this map showing the path Little Red Riding Hood took to Grandmother's house. Add trees and flowers. Show where she first met the wolf.

# Pop-Up Wolf

*Directions:* Color in the background on the pop-up page following. Then color in the wolf and the bed below. Cut it out. Follow the steps as shown to make a pop-up wolf.

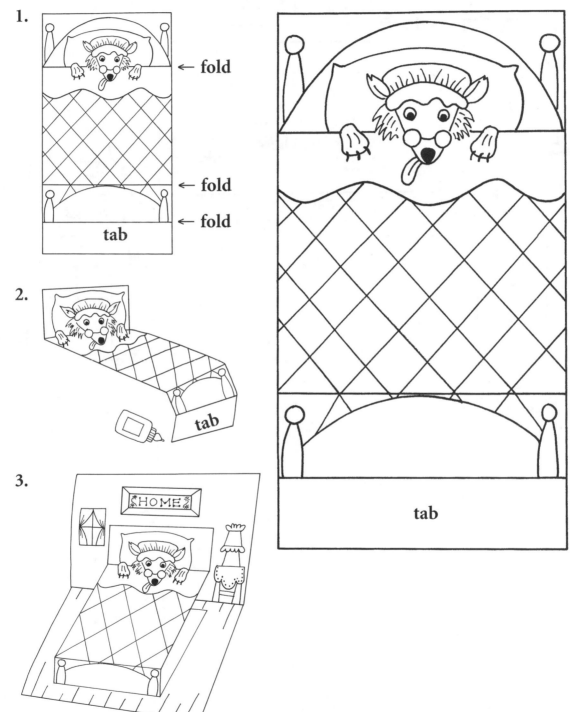

**1.**

← **fold**

← **fold**

← **fold**

**tab**

**2.**

**tab**

**3.**

HOME

**tab**

continued

glue the back of the head
of bed here

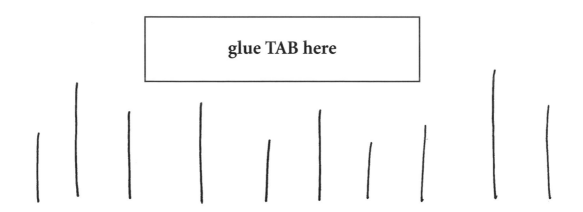

glue TAB here

Fulcrum Publishing • (800) 992-2908 • www.fulcrum-resources.com

## Little Red Pop-Up

*Directions:* First color the girl and the forest background. Then cut along the dotted line on the edge of the hood. Fold the hood forward. Glue a sheet of paper on the back to cover the back of the pop-up hood. Cut off directions. Fold in half along the vertical black line.

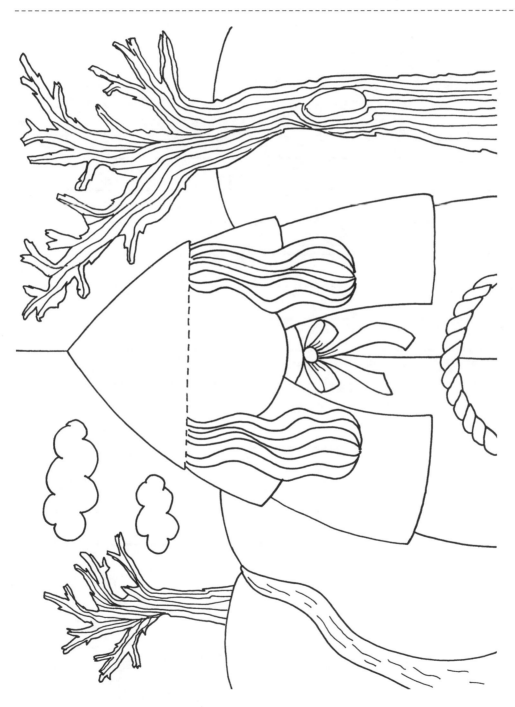

# Wolf's Letter

*Directions:* Pretend you are the wolf. Write a letter to your mom and dad telling them *your* side of the story. Then make a special envelope for your letter.

_____

_____

_____

_____

_____

_____

_____

_____

_____

_____

_____

_____

_____

## Wolf's Envelope

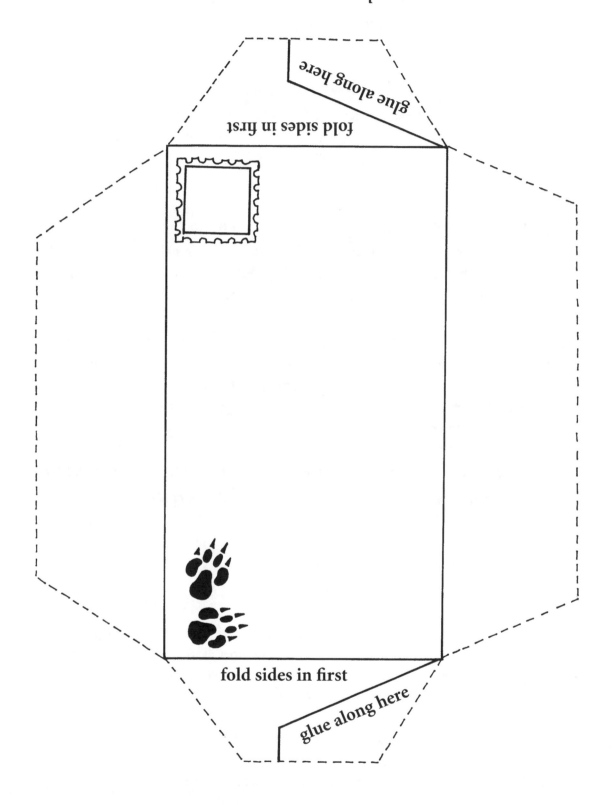

glue along here

fold sides in first

fold sides in first

glue along here

# Bibliography

Bernadette. *Little Red Riding Hood*. New York: Scholastic, 1971.

Bernadette's colorful version is available in both hardcover and paperback. Her unique illustrative style features large pages of brightly painted scenery and a small, wistful-looking Little Red Riding Hood.

De Regniers, Beatrice Schenk. *Red Riding Hood: Retold in Verse for Boys and Girls to Read to Themselves*. New York: Aladdin Books, 1972.

Now available in a sturdy paperback form, deRegniers's delightful rendition in verse should be a staple in folktale collections. Edward Gorey's red, tan, and black illustrations with their tiny details add to the charm of this classic.

du Boise, Willimae Pene. *Little Red Riding Hood*. New York: Random House, 1978.

Random House has used William Pene du Bois' lovely version for this paperback edition. Filled with full-color pages of rich green forests, a charming Little Red, a droll wolf, and a reassuring ending, this is a delightful and inexpensive book to share with children.

Eisen, Armand. *Little Red Riding Hood*. New York: Ariel Books/Alfred A. Knopf, 1988.

Lynn Bywaters Ferris illustrated this version with European charm and beauty. The book should be viewed up close to appreciate the loving detail of the pictures, which are framed with a colorful border much like the illustrative technique of Jan Brett and Trina Schart Hyman.

Goodall, John. *Little Red Riding Hood*. New York: Margaret K. McElderry Books, 1988.

This colorful, wordless picture book with its big-eyed mice as the three female characters and other assorted woodland creatures as the other characters will delight young children. Light watercolor paintings fill the book, which uses half pages to open on every other page to cleverly reveal more action. The wordless format helps youngsters develop language and sequencing skills as they use the pictures to explain the story to themselves and others.

Grimm, Jacob. *Little Red Cap*. New York: William Morrow, 1983.

Translated from the original German by Elizabeth D. Crawford and illustrated by Austrian Lisbeth Zwerger, *Little Red Cap* faithfully captures the style and mood of the original story. The realistic ink and wash and use of open space throughout the book contribute to making this a fine picture book.

Hyman, Trina Schart. *Little Red Riding Hood*. New York: Holiday House, 1983.

This award-winning version of the original tale (Caldecott Honor book) is probably the best to present to children before reading any of the variants. Hyman's retelling fleshes out the story in greater detail and builds more suspense than many of the others; however, it is the illustrations that make this book memorable. The expression of love on the grandmother's face on the first page of the book is a classic. The tiny authentic detail, unique design, and use of lush yet soft color create a feeling of rural Germany around the time of the Brothers Grimm. Give children an opportunity to peruse the book individually after it has been read to them.

McKissack, Patricia C. *Flossie and the Fox*. New York: Dial Books for Young Readers, 1986.

This African-American variant from the rural South is a delight. Told to the author as a small child by her grandfather, the clever tale begs to be read aloud. The vibrant illustrations by artist Rachel Isadora add to the enjoyment, though due to the strong oral tradition shining through, the book would be outstanding even without artwork.

Marshall, James. *Red Riding Hood*. New York: Dial Books for Young Readers, 1987.

James Marshall's rendition is not quite a parody, but a wacky romp, nevertheless. His irreverent additions, combined with his familiar, droll illustrative style, make this version a pleasure for children. (The cats are irresistible.)

Perrault, Charles. *Little Red Riding Hood*. New York: Doubleday, 1991.

Beni Montressor has illustrated the 300-year-old Perrault text that was translated from the French by George Martin. Unlike Sarah Moon's interpretation (following) that ends with Little Red being devoured, Montressor's illustrations show (but do not tell) the Grimm Brothers' ending with Little Red alive and well inside the wolf's stomach with the image of a woodcutter standing just offstage. Preview for suitability.

Perrault, Charles. *Little Red Riding Hood*. Mankato, Minn.: Creative Education, 1983.

Sarah Moon's stunning photographic version of this tale won the 1984 International Bookfair Grand Prize. Riveting, dark photographs take this story back to its origins as a cautionary tale of danger in the dark forest. It hints of the danger of sexual assault, even though the wolf depicted in shadow is a wolf and not a man.

The wolf asks Little Red to undress and get into bed with him. Though the text is faithful to the original writing and the photographic presentation is highly creative, the overall effect is intense and disturbing. Preview for suitability.

Rowland, Della. *Little Red Riding Hood/The Wolf's Tale*. New York: Carol Publishing, 1991.

While not one of the best written or illustrated versions of the tale, this *Upside Down Tale* can be used as a model for the "point of view" writing and drama activity.

Schmidt, Karen. *Little Red Riding Hood*. New York: Scholastic, 1986.

This inexpensive paperback version from Scholastic has adequate pictures by Karen Schmidt, but a choppy text. It serves the purpose of providing an easy-to-read, inexpensive book for children to read to themselves.

Wegman, William. *Little Red Riding Hood*. New York: Hyperion, 1993.

Wegman's familiar weimaraners in costume provide the illustration for this version.

Young, Ed. *Lon Po Po: A Red-Riding Hood Story from China*. New York: Putnam, 1991.

Winner of the 1990 Caldecott Award, this Chinese folktale is actually a combination of *Little Red Riding Hood* and *The Wolf and the Seven Kids*. (A good version of the latter tale is published by Silver Burdette, 1986, illustrated by Martin Ursell.) The exquisite artwork, painted in Chinese-style panels, greatly enhances the tension and mood of the story. This outstanding book is also available in paperback.

### *Parodies*

Emberly, Michael. *Ruby*. Boston: Little, Brown, 1990.

*Ruby* is an amusing parody of *Little Red Riding Hood*. It stars a little mouse girl and is filled with all kinds of animals, including a nefarious cat dressed as a shyster. Boys and girls will surely get a chuckle out of this version that has the little mouse girl pulling some clever tricks of her own.

Ernst, Lisa Campbell. *Little Red Riding Hood: A Newfangled Prairie Tale*. New York: Simon & Schuster, 1995.

Set in farm country, this delightful spoof features a spunky grandmother who opens a muffin shop and reforms the wolf.

# Chapter 2

# Turnabout Is Fair Play

## Introduction

The variants in this unit are linked by the theme of the unworthy or mean-spirited individual receiving his just desserts. Though this proverb (especially the term "turnabout") will need explanation, it aptly describes the action in the stories. All four folktales are quite different from one another and represent the unique animals, landscapes, and plants of each particular area. Class discussions comparing and contrasting the tales truly address the underlying theme of multiculturalism: so different, and yet, so similar.

### Geography

Teachers can use this unit as a springboard for teaching how to use an atlas. The countries of Tanzania (main location of the Serengeti), Burma, Mexico, and the state of Georgia in the United States can be used as locations for students to find first in the index and then locate on the appropriate maps using grid designations. Use the "Turnabout is Fair Play Map" to reinforce their learning.

### Research

The "Postage Stamp Animal Map" activity integrates basic research skills. Children look up each animal to find out where it lives and its color. Then they color the animal stamps, cut them out, and glue them into place on the map page. This activity highlights the concept that different animals are native to specific geographic areas.

### Research and Science

The "Pop-Up Animal Research" activity offers an opportunity to integrate both research skills and science into the literature curriculum. The pop-up page has space for one well-developed paragraph, though more paper could easily be glued onto the bottom of the page. If children have computer access, they could word process their report, integrating another important skill.

### Puppetry

In this unit, the highlight for children will be the "Animal Stick-Puppet Plays." The folktales are filled with dialogue and are short enough to be perfect for this activity. The drama can be improvisational or it can be presented as readers' theater with a narrator, depending on the ages and abilities of the children.

### Writing

This unit also lends itself to creative-writing activities. The "Turnabout" theme is so straightforward that children can use it as a basis for their own realistic stories with themselves as the characters. Fair play is a major concern of elementary school-aged children, which makes this a meaningful writing project. Brainstorm various crises to help children come up with ideas and also to avoid stories too heavily laden with injuries or violence.

A different creative-writing activity ties in with science. Begin by brainstorming or researching wild animals that live in your state. Create plots with larger, more powerful or deadly animals depending upon the help of weaker animals to free them. On the board or overhead, create a web of powerful, deadly animals and a different web of smaller, weaker animals. Then allow each child to pick a pair of regional animals (one from each web) to develop an animal folktale based on this plot. When the stories are complete, they can be illustrated, possibly word processed, and bound together in a class book for all to enjoy.

### Drama

For a drama activity, discuss the concept of "point of view." The tales in this unit are told from the point of view of the victimized animal. How would the stories change if the tales were told from the point of view of the aggressor or predator animal, or even from the view of the moderating or judging animal? Small groups can create a talk-show format with a moderator and three guests, each telling his side of the incident. When children are familiar with these tales, this activity is lots of fun and, at the same time, teaches the concept of point of view while building speaking skills. Brainstorm what the program might be called: Animals Who Help Too Much? Trust Issues in the Wilds?

# Simba the Lion and the Clever Trap (Africa)

Once, in the days long past, Simba the Lion was out hunting on the great plains of Africa. He smelled fresh meat and quickly made his way toward a large piece of it that, oddly enough, was attached to the end of a long pole. Wrapped around the other end of the pole was a collection of tough vine ropes. The contraption looked strange, but the fresh meat was so inviting that Simba leaped up and grabbed it in his sharp teeth. But just at that instant the end of the pole flew up, ensnaring the lion in a trap of heavy vine ropes!

"Aaah! A trap!" roared the majestic animal, thrashing about violently to escape from the clever trap. But the harder he tried to free himself, the tighter the ropes held.

Soon a family of warthogs, including a mother, a father, and four little ones, came ambling along the Serengeti Plain.

At first the father stopped the family and motioned them away from the sight of the dreaded lion. His wife, however, quickly sized up the situation and moved forward to stare at the great beast.

"Hmmm, if my eyes are not fooling me, children, I believe we have here Simba, the King of the Serengeti, caught in a simple trap," commented the mother warthog.

"I believe you are right, dear wife, but I also believe that we should move right along," said her husband, anxious that the lion just *might* find a way out of the trap.

"My dear friends, the Nguruwe (nuh go *roo* wee) family," entreated Simba most pleasantly. "Could you possibly take a few minutes to help me out of this hideous trap?"

"Oh, I don't think that would be wise, judging from your past history," answered the mother Nguruwe.

"I *certainly* would not harm you or any of your kind, if only you would release me!" pleaded the desperate lion.

"We can see that you are in a bad situation, and we feel badly about that," admitted the father warthog, who was a kindhearted animal, "but frankly, we don't trust you, and we have our own family to think about."

"I don't blame you a bit," agreed Simba, "but I will change my ways. Surely, you cannot walk away and leave a fellow animal to suffer?"

"Very well," answered the father Nguruwe, who along with his family pulled and tugged on the vines until Simba was able to shake loose from their hold.

"Thank you, thank you, Nguruwe family!" cried Simba gratefully. "Now I need to continue on my hunt."

"We too need to search for food," said the father Nguruwe as the animals parted in opposite directions to search for their next meal.

The animals had not gone too far when Simba suddenly turned around and scampered back to catch up with the Nguruwe family.

"Father Nguruwe, I just thought of something!" said Simba. "Here I am, more hungry than ever after my ordeal with the trap, and here you are with this huge family of four children. Why don't you simply give me one of your little ones to eat? That would solve my problem and with so many children, you won't miss just one."

"You know, Simba," interrupted the mother warthog, who had quickly decided that someone other than her kindly husband should handle the situation, "I was just thinking about that trap back there. For the life of me, I can't imagine how an animal of your cunning could *ever* have been trapped in such a simple device."

"Well!" returned Simba indignantly. "It's because you didn't see how cleverly that trap was designed and concealed. Why it could have trapped *any* animal going near it."

"Really?" replied the mother warthog skeptically. "It didn't seem that clever to me at the time."

"Then let us go back to it, and I will show you that it was an exceedingly clever trap that *no* animal could possibly have avoided!" said Simba, now greatly annoyed by the insinuations being made by the mother Nguruwe.

So the animals traveled back to the trap.

"See, look at this pole and these vines!" said Simba as he walked around the trap, pointing to various features with his huge paw.

"I still don't understand," said the mother Nguruwe innocently. "Show me exactly how it worked."

So Simba stepped between the rope vines, and the warthogs quickly released the pole. Snap! The vines instantly entrapped the lion once again.

"There, so now you can see that any animal, even the King of the Serengeti, could be caught in this clever trap! Now, let me out so we can continue our conversation," said Simba, glad to have proven his point.

"No, we won't release you this time," answered the wise Nguruwe parents, "because we love all our children equally and cannot part with even one of them."

"I demand that you release me this instant!" roared Simba imperiously.

"Your demand is not our command," answered the Nguruwe couple as they headed across the Serengeti with their four little warthogs.

# Kho and the Tiger (Burma)

nce upon a time there was a young Burmese boy named Kho who loved the animals of the forest and spent much of his time in their company. But the animal he loved best of all was the beautiful tiger. They often walked together through the heavy forest, though the tiger, unlike the boy, had something other than friendship on his mind. The tiger hoped that the boy would allow him to accompany him back to the village where the tiger could then kill and eat one of the villager's plump calves. Kho never invited the tiger into the clearing near the village for he knew that the villagers considered the tiger a dreaded enemy.

One day after a particularly friendly walk together, the tiger begged Kho to allow him to walk home with him.

"Come on, Kho, surely you are not ashamed of being seen with such a fine friend as myself?" asked the tiger indignantly.

"Oh, no, it is not that," assured Kho. "It is only that the villagers are afraid of you and would not like the idea of my bringing you in so close to them."

"Very well," sniffed the tiger indignantly. "I will meet you tomorrow at the same place in the forest."

So Kho ran on ahead to the clearing and then to his house, while he assumed the tiger went on back deeper into the forest. The tiger, however, crept into some underbrush and waited until the villagers were all sound asleep. Then he silently stalked a fat young calf, killed it, and dragged it off into the forest to eat.

When Kho awakened the next morning, the village was in an uproar.

"Tiger attack! Tiger attack!" shouted the distraught villagers, frightened that a predatory animal had been so close. "We will set a trap that will put an end to his killing!"

Kho was frightened for his friend and ran back into the forest as soon as he could make his escape.

"My dear tiger, why did you ignore my advice?" asked the boy grimly. "Do not ever come back to the village again or they will surely kill you."

The tiger, full of food and confidence, replied, "I am afraid of no one, boy. I'll do *exactly* as I please."

No amount of pleading would change the animal's mind, so Kho finally left the tiger and ran back to his village.

Late that night the village awoke to a terrible roaring. It was the tiger, caught in the trap that the villagers had set for him. The villagers were overjoyed to have trapped the wily animal that struck so much fear into their hearts. But as the day went by and the animal's roar grew faint from hunger and thirst, Kho's heart went out to his friend. So he went to visit him.

"Dear friend, I cannot bear to see you suffer," said Kho to the entrapped tiger, but if I set you free, you would probably kill another calf and the the village would blame me."

"Why, not at all," assured the tiger. "If I could get out of here, I would head back into the deepest part of the forest and never come back again."

Kho doubted the cocky tiger, but as the days went by, the kindhearted boy could bear it no longer. Late one night, as the animal neared the end of its life, Kho crept out of his bed and came to the rescue of the tiger in the trap.

"Now remember, if I set you free, you must leave here immediately and not come back," said the boy solemnly.

"Of course, of course, hurry up," answered the tiger impatiently.

By twisting ropes and vines this way and that, Kho was finally able to set the large tiger free.

"Now before I leave, I *do* need some nourishment," said the weakened tiger, "and you will do."

"Me?" exclaimed the astonished boy. "After I warned you repeatedly not to come here and then you ignored my warnings and was trapped and I freed you? Don't you owe me some gratitude?"

"Gratitude?" replied the tiger. "There is no such thing."

"There is so!" said Kho angrily.

"Then let us put this to a third party," answered the tiger.

"Very well, let us ask the rabbit, as she is the wisest of all animals," said Kho as he helped the unsteady animal walk away from the village clearing and into the forest.

They soon encountered a rabbit and each side explained his version of the story.

"So, what do you think?" asked Kho and the tiger together.

"I can't make a decision without first seeing where all this took place," said the rabbit. "Can you both take me back to the trap in the village?"

"Of course," answered the boy and the tiger in unison.

After a short walk the three animals came to the trap at the edge of the village clearing.

"Tiger, could you be so kind as to once again get into the trap so I can see what the situation was when the boy decided to free you?" asked the rabbit.

"Certainly," replied the tiger as he climbed back into the trap, knowing the rabbit would soon agree that there was no such thing as gratitude.

"Now, is this exactly where both of you were positioned before this dispute developed?" asked the rabbit.

"Yes," answered the boy and the tiger together.

"Very well, I will leave the two of you settle it then," said the rabbit as she scurried away into the forest, leaving the two surprised individuals standing there.

Kho and the tiger turned slowly and looked at one another silently for a couple of minutes. Then Kho turned and ran back to his home in the village and the tiger died later that night.

# Señor Coyote and the Tricked Trickster (Mexico)

One day long ago in Mexico's land of sand and giant cactus *Señor* Coyote and *Señor* Mouse had a quarrel.

None now alive can remember why, but recalling what spirited *caballeros* these two were, I suspect that it was some small thing that meant little.

Be that as it may, these two took their quarrels seriously and for a long time would not speak to each other.

Then one day Mouse found Señor Coyote caught in a trap. He howled and twisted and fought, but he could not get out. He had just about given up when he saw Señor Mouse grinning at him.

"Mouse! *Mi viejo amigo*—my old friend!" he cried. "Please gnaw this leather strap in two and get me out of this trap."

"But we are no longer friends," Mouse said. "We have quarreled, remember?"

"Nonsense!" Señor Coyote cried. "Why I love you better than I do Rattlesnake, Owl, or anybody in the desert. You must gnaw me loose. And please hurry for if the *peon* catches me I will wind up a fur rug on his wife's kitchen floor."

Mouse remembered how mean Señor Coyote had been to him. He was always playing tricks on Mouse and his friends. They were very funny to Señor Coyote for he was a great trickster, but they often hurt little Mouse.

"I'd like to gnaw you free," he said, "but I am old and my teeth tire easily."

"Really, Señor Mouse, you are ungrateful," said Señor Coyote reproachfully. "Remember all the nice things I have done for you."

"What were they?"

"Why —" Coyote began and stopped. He was unable to think of a single thing. There was good reason for this. He had done nothing for Mouse but trick him.

But Señor Coyote is a sly fellow. He said quickly, "Oh, why remind you of them. You remember them all."

"I fear my memory of yesterday is too dim," Mouse said, "but I could remember very well what you could do for me tomorrow."

"Tomorrow?" Coyote asked.

"Yes, tomorrow. If I gnaw away the leather rope holding you in the trap, what will you do for me tomorrow, and the day after tomorrow and the day after tomorrow and the day—"

"Stop!" Señor Coyote cried. "How long is this going on?"

"A life is worth a life. If I save your life, you should work for me for a lifetime. That is the only fair thing to do."

"But everyone would laugh at a big, brave, smart fellow like me working as a slave for a mere mouse!" Señor Coyote cried.

"Is that worse than feeling sad for you because your hide is a rug in the peon's kitchen?"

Señor Coyote groaned and cried and argued, but finally agreed when he saw that Mouse would not help him otherwise.

"Very well," he said tearfully, "I agree to work for you until either of us die or until I have a chance to get even by saving your life."

Mouse said with a sly grin, "That is very fine, but I remember what a great trickster you are. So you must also promise that as soon as I free you that you will not jump on me, threaten to kill me, and then save my life by letting me go!"

"Why, how can you suggest such a thing!" Coyote cried indignantly. And then to himself he added, "This mouse is getting *too* smart!"

"Very well, promise," Mouse retorted.

"But I am not made for work," Señor Coyote said tearfully. "I live by being sly."

"Then be sly and get out of the trap yourself," Mouse retorted.

"Very well," Señor Coyote said sadly. "I will work for you until I can pay back the debt of my life."

And so Mouse gnawed the leather strap in two and Coyote was saved. Then for many days thereafter Señor Coyote worked for Mouse. Mouse was very proud to have the famous Señor Coyote for a servant. Señor Coyote was greatly embarrassed since he did not like being a servant and disliked working even more.

There was nothing he could do since he had given his promise. He worked all day and dreamed all night of how he could trick his way out of his troubles. He could think of nothing.

Then one day Baby Mouse came running to him. "My father has been caught by Señor Snake!" he cried. "Please come and save him."

"Hooray!" cried Coyote. "If I save him, I will be released from my promise to work for him."

He went out to the desert rocks and found Señor Rattlesnake with his coils around Señor Mouse.

"Please let him go and I will catch you two more mice," Coyote said.

"My wise old mother used to tell me that a bird in hand is worth two in the bush," Snake replied. "By the same reasoning, one mouse in Snake's stomach is worth two in Coyote's mind."

"Well, I tried, Mouse," Coyote said. "I'm sorry you must be eaten."

"But you must save me, then you will be free from your promise to me," Mouse said.

"If you're eaten, I'll be free anyway," Coyote said.

"Then everyone will say that Coyote was not smart enough to trick Snake," Mouse said quickly. "And I think they will be right. It makes me very sad for I always thought Señor Coyote the greatest trickster in the world."

This made Coyote's face turn red. He we very proud that everyone thought him so clever. Now he just *had* to save Mouse.

So he said to Snake, "How did you catch Mouse anyway?"

A rock rolled on top of him and he was trapped," Mouse said. "He asked me to help him roll it off. When I did he jumped on me before I could run away."

"That is not true," Snake said. "How could a little mouse have the strength to roll away a big rock. There is the rock. Now you tell me if you think Mouse could roll it."

It was a very big rock and Coyote admitted that Mouse could not possibly have budged it.

"But it is like the story *Mamacita* tells her children at bedtime," Mouse said quickly. "Once there was a poor burro who had a load of hay just as large as he could carry. His master added just one more straw and the poor burro fell in the dirt. Snake did not have quite enough strength to push the rock off himself. I came along and was like that last straw on the burro's back and together we rolled the rock away."

"Maybe that is true," Snake said, "but by Mouse's own words, he did only very little of the work. So I owe him only a very little thanks. That is not enough to keep me from eating him."

"Hmmm," said Coyote. "Now you understand, Snake, that I do not care what happens myself. If Mouse is eaten, I will be free of my bargain anyway. I am only thinking of your own welfare for both of us. I don't need your thoughts."

"Thank you," said Señor Ratlesnake, "but I do enough thinking about my welfare for both of us. I don't need your thoughts."

"Nevertheless," Coyote insisted, "everyone is going to say that you ate Mouse after he was kind enough to help you."

"I don't care," Snake said. "Nobody says anything good of me anyway."

"Well," said Coyote, "I'll tell you what we should do. We should put everything back as it was. Then I will see for myself if Mouse was as much help as he said he was or as little as you claim. Then I can tell everyone that you were right, Snake."

"Very well," said Señor Snake. "I was lying like this and the rock was on me—"

"Like this?" Coyote said, quickly rolling the rock across Snake's body.

"Ouch!" said Snake. "That is right."

"Can you get out?" Coyote asked.

"No," said Snake.

"Then turn Mouse loose and let him push," said Coyote.

This Snake did, but before Mouse could push, Coyote said, "But on second thought if Mouse pushes, you would then grab him again and we'd be back arguing. Since you are both as you were before the argument started, let us leave it a that and all be friends again!"

Then Coyote turned to Mouse. "So, my friend, I have now saved your life. We are now even and my debt to you is paid."

"But mine is such a *little* life," Mouse protested. "And yours is so much *larger*. I don't think they balance. You should still pay me part."

"This is ridiculous!" Coyote cried. "I—"

"Wait" Snake put in hopefully. "Let me settle the quarrel. Now you roll the rock away. I'll take Mouse in my coils just the way we were when Coyote came up. We'll be then in a position to decide if—"

"Thank you," said Mouse. "It isn't necessary to trouble everyone again. Señor Coyote, we are even."

# Brer Possum and Brer Snake (United States, African-American)

 ne frosty morning Brer Possum was going down the road attending to his own business, when he came across Brer Snake lying in the road with a brick on his back. Now, Brer Snake is a dangerous creature; he'll bite you if you don't watch out.

So Brer Possum walked around Brer Snake. But then he heard Brer Snake holler out, "Oh, Brer Possum—please, sir—don't leave me here to die. Can't you see the brick on my back? Please lift it off."

Brer Possum looked around, and he looked at Brer Snake, and then he reached down and picked the brick right off Brer Snake's back. And then he went on down the road attending to his own business.

But again Brer Snake cried out. "Oh, Brer Possum, don't leave me in the road to die. Don't you see how cold I am? I'm so cold I can't crawl. Pick me up and put me in your pocket, please, sir. You have a warm pocket right there in front."

Brer Possum came back and got Brer Snake and stuck him in his pocket, and then he went on down the road.

All of a sudden Brer Snake stuck his head out of the pocket and said, "I'm going to bite you; I'm going to bite you."

Brer Possum cried, "Why are you going to bite me, Brer Snake? I haven't done anything wrong to you. In fact, I helped you. I lifted the brick off your back, and I stuck you in my pocket."

Brer Snake said, "I don't know. I guess it's just my nature to bite."

Brer Possum sighed. "Well, if I'm going to die, Brer Snake, let me go down to Brer Rabbit's house and tell him good-bye."

"All right," said Brer Snake.

So Brer Possum went down to Brer Rabbit's house. Brer Rabbit was sitting on his front piazza, just a-rocking back and forth. And he called out, "Hello there, Brer Possum."

"Good morning, Brer Rabbit," answered Brer Possum.

"Where are you going?" asked Brer Rabbit.

Brer Rabbit said, "I'm not going anywhere. I just came to tell you good-bye because I'm going to die—that's all."

"My goodness, what's the matter with you?" asked Brer Rabbit.

"I've got a snake in my pocket."

"Oh, my!" said Brer Rabbit. "What're you doing with a snake in your pocket? Don't you know he's a dangerous creature?"

"Yes, I know that now, sir."

"Well, what happened?" asked Brer Rabbit.

And then Brer Possum told Brer Rabbit how he had taken the brick off Brer Snake's back and picked him up and stuck him in his pocket, and how Brer Snake had said he was going to bite him.

Brer Rabbit said, "I can't understand that. Is that right, Brer Snake?"

Brer Snake stuck his head out of Brer Possum's pocket and said, "Yes, that's right."

Brer Rabbit shook his head all puzzled-like. "Let's go down where the thing happened, and then maybe I can understand. I can't understand it now."

So the three of them went down the road together. When they reached the brick, Brer Rabbit stepped over beside it, and then he said, "Brer Possum, where were you standing?"

"Right here," answered Brer Possum.

"And, Brer Snake, where were you standing?"

Brer Snake crawled out of Brer Possum's pocket over to the brick and said, "Right here."

Quickly Brer Rabbit slapped the brick down on Brer Snake's back, and jumped away. Then he said, "Now, you just stay there, Brer Snake. That's where poison creatures belong. And you, Brer Possum, don't you ever trouble trouble, until trouble troubles you!"

# Discussion Questions

### Prereading Questions

- What is The Golden Rule? How is it like "turnabout is fair play?"

- Many cultures have sayings and folktales dealing with fairness. Why do you think this is so?

### Reading Focus Question

- In times long ago, folktales were shared with adults and children alike, though some stories appealed more to children than others. The following stories appeal especially to children because they have animal characters, are easy to understand, and are fairly short. As you listen to them, think about why parents may have wanted to tell these tales to their children.

### Post-Reading Questions

- (Return to Focus Question) Why do you think parents may have wanted to tell these tales to their children?

- Which two stories had a rabbit as the wise character? Are rabbits generally considered highly intelligent animals? Why do you think the original storytellers chose a rabbit for the wise character? What animal is usually portrayed as the wise animal of the forest? Is that animal intelligent?

- Each folktale had a Good Samaritan character. What does that mean? Who was the Good Samaritan in each folktale? How did each Good Samaritan character feel at first about the animal in distress? In each case, what caused him to change his mind?

- In each story a character convinced the animal in distress to replay the entire rescue scene. Who was that animal in each folktale? Do you think that animal really had no idea what had happened? Then why did they set up the replay?

- Which characters in these folktales learned lessons? What did they learn?

- These folktales are remarkably similar and yet come from cultures geographically far apart. How many children think that all of these folktales came from the same tale? How many children think that they developed separately in the different cultures? (There is no correct answer, but one should have a reason for choosing a particular theory.)

# Turnabout Is Fair Play Map

*Directions:* Find the continent for each folktale. Choose a colored pencil or fine-tipped marker to color both the continent and the matching box in the legend.

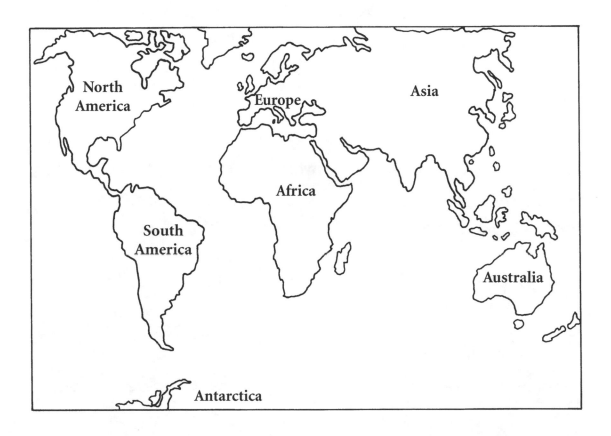

☐ Africa ("Simba the Lion and the Clever Trap")

☐ Burma ("Kho and the Tiger")

☐ Mexico ("Señor Coyote and the Tricked Trickster")

☐ United States ("Brer Possum and Brer Snake")

# Postage Stamp Animal Map

*Directions:* Color the animal stamps. Then cut them out. Glue each stamp onto the correct square on the map on the following page.

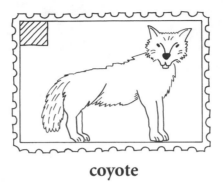

**coyote**

**warthog**

**opossum**

**rattlesnake**

**rabbit**

**tiger**

**lion**

continued

## Postage Stamp Animal Map (continued)

```
Asia

Europe
Africa

Australia

North
America

South
America

Antarctica
```

| warthog |
|---------|

| tiger |
|-------|

| rattlesnake |
|-------------|

| rabbit |
|--------|

| opossum |
|---------|

| lion |
|------|

| coyote |
|--------|

# Pop-Up Animal Research

*Directions:* Use an encyclopedia to look up information about an interesting animal from the folktales. Write your report on the lines. The top half of the paper will be the background. Draw scenery that is accurate for your animal's environment. On a separate piece of paper, draw and cut out your animal. Cut along the dotted lines and fold forward before gluing on your cut-out animal. Fold top half of paper forward along the black line in the center.

- - - - - - - - - - - - - - - - - - - - - - - - - - - - - - - - - - - - - - - - - - - - - - - - - - - - -

**Animal:** _____

**Glue figure
of animal
here**

_____

_____

_____

_____

_____

_____

_____

_____

_____

_____

**Resource:**

Fulcrum Publishing • (800) 992-2908 • www.fulcrum-resources.com

# Animal Stick-Puppet Plays

*Directions:* Choose an animal folktale to present. Color the animals needed for your play. Glue them onto tag board. Cut them out. Glue a stick to the back. Practice your play with other actors. Then use a table turned on its side as a puppet stage to create an exciting performance for the class!

continued

# Bibliography

Faulkner, William J. *Brer Tiger and the Big Wind*. New York: Morrow Junior Books, 1995.

Clever Brer Rabbit saves the animals from starvation by tricking selfish, self-centered Brer Tiger in this single-tale picture book beautifully illustrated by Roberta Wilson.

Harris, Joel Chandler. *Jump on Over! The Adventures of Brer Rabbit and His Family*. New York: Harcourt Brace Jovanovich, 1989.

No longer a bachelor, Brer Rabbit has married Miss Molly and they now have seven little "rabs" and more hilarious adventures.

Hayward, Linda. *All Stuck Up*. New York: Random House, 1990.

Lively, colorful illustrations are used to create a beginning-to-read story of "Tar Baby" in a paperback edition for the youngest reader.

Lester, Julius. *The Tales of Uncle Remus: The Adventures of Brer Rabbit*. New York: Dial, 1987.

Jerry Pinkney's whimsical drawings of the animals complement this excellent story collection retold by Julius Lester.

———. *More Tales of Uncle Remus: The Adventures of Brer Rabbit, His Friends, Enemies, and Others*. New York: Dial, 1988.

More delightful tales about Brer Rabbit and all the animals of the forest. Both full-color and black-and-white drawings by Jerry Pinkney add appeal to this story collection.

———. *Further Tales of Uncle Remus: The Misadventures of Brer Rabbit, Brer Fox, Brer Wolf, the Doodang, and Other Creatures*. New York: Dial, 1990.

Third in the set of multiple award-winning Brer Rabbit folktale books, this addition provides even more delightful stories for children to read to themselves or to listen to adults read them aloud.

————. *The Last Tales of Uncle Remus.* New York: Dial, 1994.

The final collection is different from the other three in that it contains mostly pourquoi tales, rather than humorous stories.

Makhanlall, David P. *Brer Anansi and the Boat Race.* London: Blackie and Son Ltd., 1988.

Though Brer Rabbit is featured in this rollicking folktale from the Caribbean, it is Brer Anansi who is the main character and has the last laugh. Vividly colored, humorous full-page illustrations by Amelia Rosato make this a delightful book for younger children.

Parks, Van Dyke, and Malcolm Jones. *Jump! The Adventures of Brer Rabbit.* New York: Harcourt Brace Jovanovich, 1986.

Van Dyke Parks and Malcolm Jones have adapted the old Brer Rabbit tales with warm humor and a feel for the pace and speech of the old South. Barry Moser's illustrations capture the character of the familiar cast of animals.

————. *Jump Again! More Adventures of Brer Rabbit.* New York: Harcourt Brace Jovanovich, 1987.

After receiving the critical acclaim generated by the publication of *Jump!*, the pair teamed up to create this continuation (not necessarily a sequel).

Weiss, Jaqueline Shachter. *Young Brer Rabbit and Other Trickster Tales from the Americas.* Owings Mills, Md.: Stemmer House, 1985.

This unique collection features Brer Rabbit tales from Central and South America. Though not as familiar to Americans as the Uncle Remus tales, these folktales were also brought to the various countries of the Americas by African slaves. Colorful illustrations by Clinton Arrowood add to this fine collection.

# Chapter 3

# Don't Believe
# Everything You Hear

## Introduction

The large quantity of variants (plus their short length and repetitive nature) makes this unit ideal for cooperative-learning groups. The six folktales provide a tale for every four or five children to use in a variety of activities. The English tale "HennyPenny/Chicken Little" is readily available in attractive picture books (see Bibliography on pages 46–47).

### *Geography*

Because these tales are from all over the world, they provide an opportunity to use a globe or an atlas to integrate geography into the study of literature. Have children locate the country of origin in an atlas index, then use the grid key to find that country on the map. Use the "Don't Believe Everything You Hear Map" to reinforce their learning.

### *Understanding Cumulative Literature*

The activity "Character Chains" teaches the concept of cumulative literature, which means that the action builds and repeats, finally coming to a quick or surprising conclusion. In addition to the five folktales in this unit, many old nursery rhymes and songs are structured this way, such as "Old MacDonald Had a Farm" and the Danish folktale "The Fat Cat." Another great example is the hilarious book *The House That Jack Built* by Janet Stevens (Holiday House, 1985). To help children develop oral storytelling skills with these stories, have them create a set of chains to use as a prop. Use the reproducible or create links from any type or size paper.

### Art

The "Accordion Book" activity yields a marvelous product—a set of illustrated folktale books for the class. Because of the amount of work and time involved, this project is ideal for cooperative-learning groups. Each group can divide up the parts of the story to rewrite, illustrate, and assemble, since there will be one story on the front side of the book and a different story on the back. This requires planning so that the book ends evenly. The problem solving and logistics of this activity present a real-life challenge to children, who enjoy producing lasting items for their classroom. It is helpful to laminate the final product or they eventually fall apart due to repeated folding.

### Drama

Because of the action, dialogue, and shear silliness of some of these tales, they lend themselves to drama activities, and can be presented to the younger children in the school. Have students rewrite the story as a play. It can be difficult to find drama activities that involve everyone; these tales are filled with so many different animals that there should be enough parts for the entire class.

### Grammar

The abundant dialogue in these folktales provides an opportunity for children to work with quotation marks. Choose a representative page of dialogue, photocopy it, and "white out" the quotation marks. Then either duplicate copies for each individual or make an overhead transparency for group instruction.

# Who Can You Believe? (Africa)

nce a farmer went out to his field to dig up yams. His sharp digging stick poked into the side of a yam.

"Leave me alone!" cried the yam.

The farmer stood in amazement, looking in every direction to discover the source of the voice.

"You heard her," said the man's dog. "The yam wants you to leave her alone."

At this the man became very angry because he had never heard his dog speak before, especially in such a sharp tone. So he broke a branch off a tree to hit the dog.

"Leave me alone!" cried the tree.

The farmer was so astonished that he quickly threw the branch down. It landed on a flat stone nearby.

"Leave me alone!" cried the stone.

This was too much for the bewildered farmer, and he started running on down the road away from his fields.

A fisherman carrying a net of fish was walking along the roadway and was startled by the sight of the running farmer.

"What is the matter?" asked the fisherman.

"First my yam tells me to leave her alone, and then my dog agrees with her. Then both a tree and a stone scold me," explained the farmer.

"Really?" answered the incredulous fisherman.

"What did he do to the yam in the first place?" asked the fish in the net.

"Aaaah!" shrieked the astounded farmer and the fisherman upon hearing a fish speak.

They raced down the road and presently came upon a weaver carrying a bundle of cloth.

"What is the matter?" asked the weaver.

The farmer and the fisherman stopped in the road and the farmer began to explain, "First my yam tells me to leave her alone and then my dog agrees with her. Then both a tree and stone scold me."

"I don't see that that is cause to become so excited," replied the weaver in a calm voice.

"You'd think differently if it happened to you!" exclaimed the weaver's bundle of cloth.

"Aaaah!" shrieked the farmer, the fisherman, and the weaver as they raced away together down the road.

At last the three men reached the village, where they decided to consult the chief about their extraordinary morning.

A servant brought out a ceremonial chair and the chief sat down upon it. The three men sat down and the farmer began his story, "First my yam tells me to leave her alone and then my dog agrees with her. Then both a tree and a stone scold me."

Then the fisherman chimed in, "And the fish in my net asked what the farmer had done to the yam in the first place!"

Finally, the weaver added, "My bundle of cloth called out, 'You'd think differently if it happened to you!'"

At first the chief listened to these tales patiently, but as they became more fantastic, a scowl crept across his face.

"This is absolutely preposterous! Go back to your work immediately and forget all about this," admonished the chief.

The three men arose and walked away from the chief.

As they disappeared down the road, the chief stood and turned around to take the ceremonial chair back into his dwelling.

As he picked up the chair, he shook his head and mumbled under his breath, "What nonsense those men were spouting."

"Incredible, wasn't it?" answered the ceremonial chair. "A talking yam, of all things!"

# Mr. Louse and Mrs. Louse (Belgium)

Mr. Louse and Mrs. Louse lived in a little house, and one day Mrs. Louse had to go shopping. She said, "While I am gone, Mr. Louse, please make the soup for our dinner." In doing so, he leaned too far over the pot, fell in, and was knocked senseless. When Mrs. Louse returned, she could not find Mr. Louse anywhere. At last she looked into the pot and there she saw him. She shrieked loudly and started to weep.

A passing dog asked her why she wept and she replied, "How can I help it? My husband is drowned in the soup pot, and so I weep." The dog began to bark loudly.

The cart in the dooryard asked the dog, "Why do you bark?" and the dog replied, "How can I help it? Mr. Louse is drowned in the soup pot, and Mrs. Louse is weeping, and so I bark." The cart started rolling backwards and ran into a tree.

The tree asked the cart, "Why do you roll backwards?" and the cart replied, "How can I help it? Mr. Louse is drowned in the soup pot, and Mrs. Louse is weeping, and the dog is barking, and so I roll backwards." The tree began to grow very small.

A bird asked the tree, "Why do you grow small?" and the tree replied, "How can I help it? Mr. Louse is drowned in the soup pot, and Mrs. Louse is weeping, and the dog is barking, and the cart is rolling backwards, and so I grow small." The bird began to pluck out its feathers.

A boy carrying pots to fetch water asked the bird, "Why do you pluck out your feathers?" and the bird replied, "How can I help it? Mr. Louse is drowned in the soup pot, and Mrs. Louse is weeping, and the dog is barking, and the cart is rolling backwards, and the tree is growing small, and so I pluck out my feathers." The boy began to break his pots.

The boy's father saw this and asked, "Why do you break your pots?" and the boy replied, "How can I help it? Mr. Louse is drowned in the soup pot, and Mrs. Louse is weeping, and the dog is barking, and the cart is rolling backwards, and the tree is growing small, and the bird is plucking out its feathers, and so I break my pots."

The father was so annoyed at hearing all this nonsense that he gave a good drubbing to the boy, who threw a stone at the bird, who began to peck the tree, which gave a big shove to the cart, which ran over the foot of the dog, who, with a crunch, bit Mrs. Louse in two. Just then, Mr. Louse regained his senses and crawled out of the pot. Seeing that Mrs. Louse was dead, he thought, "Well, that's a pity!" and he ate up all the soup.

# The Day the Sky Fell (Germany)

nce a boy decided to go play in a pasture. Suddenly he began to run, and soon he came to a little duck. The little duck said, "Little boy, why are you running?"

"Oh, oh! the sky is going to fall."

"Little boy, who told you so?"

"A little piece of it fell on my little shin."

The little duck started running with him. In a while they came to a little goose, who said, "Why are you running?" The little duck said, "Oh, oh! the sky is going to fall."

"Little duck, who told you so?"

"The little boy told me."

"Little boy, who told *you*?"

"A little piece of it fell on my little shin."

The little goose started running with them. In a while they came to a little dog, who said, "Why are you running?" The little goose said, "Oh, oh! the sky is going to fall."

"Little goose, who told you so?"

"The little duck told me."

"Little duck, who told *you*?"

"The little boy told me."

"Little boy, who told *you*?"

"A little piece of it fell on my little shin."

The little dog started running with them. In a while they came to a little colt, who said, "Why are you running?" The little dog said, "Oh, oh! the sky is going to fall."

"Little dog, who told you so?"

"The little goose told me."

"Little goose, who told *you*?"

"The little duck told me."

"Little duck, who told *you*?"

"The little boy told me."

"Little boy, who told *you*?"

"A little piece of it fell on my little shin."

The little colt started running with them. In a while they came to a little calf, who said, "Why are you running?" The little colt said, "Oh, oh! the sky is going to fall."

"Little colt, who told you so?"

"The little dog told me."

"Little dog, who told *you*?

"The little goose told me."

"Little goose, who told *you*?"

"The little duck told me."

"Little duck, who told *you*?"

"The little boy told me."

"Little boy, who told *you*?"

"A little piece of it fell on my little shin."

The little calf started running with them. In a while they came to a little beaver, who said, "Why are you running?" They all cried out , "Oh, oh! the sky is going to fall."

"How do you know?"

"A little piece of it has already fallen on the little boy's little shin!"

The little beaver took them with him under a cherry tree. He shook the tree and cherries fell on all of them. Then he said:

"Look, you foolish animals! The little boy walked under a cherry tree and a stem fell on his little shin. From this he thought the sky was going to fall."

The animals felt so ashamed that they all started running away from each other. They are still running, and if you catch one you can have it.

# The Hare and the Rumor (India)

nce a small hare sat under a fruit tree thinking.

"Earthquakes are frightening. They cause the earth to shake and tremble and, finally, parts of the earth break apart. I wonder what I should do if an earthquake should start?" pondered the little hare to himself.

As the hare was worrying about this, a ripe piece of fruit fell with a heavy thud just behind him.

"Horrors! It has started! The great earthquake that I was fearing has begun!" the hare shouted aloud.

Quickly he started running around in circles and then sprinted away toward the ocean. On the way he passed another hare.

"What's the matter?" called the hare.

"It's a giant earthquake! Run for your life!" called the first hare to his friend.

So the second hare started running toward the ocean also. Other hares heard the alarm and soon thousands were racing for their lives. The news spread and other species, in turn, sounded the alarm and headed toward the ocean to avoid the great earthquake. The deer, boars, elk, buffaloes, oxen, rhinoceroses, tigers, and elephants all thundered across the Indian terrain.

The clouds of dust and din of the animals awakened a lion in his cave. He looked out of his cave in the hillside to see vast herds of animals in flight.

"What is happening? Where are all the animals going?" asked the lion. When his companion told him that the animals were running from a great earthquake that would break apart the earth, he became deeply worried.

"They are headed straight toward the ocean. If they aren't stopped, they'll all be drowned!" he cried.

The lion raced down the slope to the front of the animal herds and roared the loudest, most frightening roar he could muster. This immediately stopped the animals in their tracks.

"What is the problem here?" the lion fiercely demanded.

"The earth is breaking! The earth is breaking!" cried the hysterical animals.

"This doesn't sound very logical. Let's talk to the largest animals first," reasoned the lion calmly. "Elephants, elephants, tell me what is going on."

"The earth is breaking up from an earthquake," answered the elephants.

"Who told you this?" asked the lion.

"The tigers told us," answered the elephants.

"The rhinoceroses told us," answered the tigers.

"The oxen told us," answered the rhinoceroses.

"The buffaloes told us," answered the oxen.

"The elk told us," answered the buffaloes.

"The boars told us," answered the elk.

"The hares told us," answered the boars.

"The little hare told us," answered the hares.

"Is this true," asked the lion to the small hare, "that you told the animals that the earth was breaking up?"

"Oh, yes," answered the little hare, "I heard it with my own ears."

"Where?" asked the lion.

"Under the tree where I live," answered the hare assuredly.

"Hop on my back and take me to the place where this happened," said the lion. "The rest of you animals wait here for my verdict."

With that the lion raced away toward the hare's home with the little hare clinging to the lion's back.

"There!" shouted the little hare. "Under that big tree just ahead."

The lion walked cautiously under the tree and searched carefully, but the only thing he could find was a large, very ripe piece of fruit.

"This must have been the cause of all this—a piece of fruit falling to the ground," said the lion as he turned to race back to the waiting animals.

When he returned, he said to the animals, "It was only ripe fruit falling to the ground. The earth is not breaking up, nor is there an earthquake. I ask you animals now, which is worse: the one who starts a rumor or the one who believes it?"

# The Cock and the Hen (Russia)

nce there lived a cock and a hen, and one day they went to the woods to get nuts. When they got to the grove of nut trees, the cock climbed up to throw down the nuts and the hen stayed down on the ground to pick them up. The cock threw down a little nut that fell into the little hen's eye and knocked it out. She ran away crying. Some lords rode by and asked:

"Little hen, little hen, why are you crying?"

"Because the little cock knocked out my eye."

"Little cock, little cock, why did you knock out the little hen's eye?"

"Because the nut tree tore my breeches."

"Nut tree, nut tree, why did you tear the cock's breeches?"

"Because the goats were gnawing my bark."

"Goats, goats, why did you gnaw the nut tree's bark?"

"Because the shepherds do not take care of us."

"Shepherds, shepherds, why don't you take care of the goats?"

"Because the farmer's wife does not feed us pancakes."

"Farmer's wife, farmer's wife, why don't you feed the shepherds pancakes?"

"Because my sow spilled my dough."

"Sow, sow, why did you spill the dough?"

"Because the wolf carried off my little pig."

"Wolf, wolf, why did you carry off the sow's little pig?"

"I was hungry and God commanded me to eat."

# Discussion Questions

### Prereading Questions

🔸 The following folktales are filled with repetition. What does repetition in stories mean? Can you give an example?

🔸 These tales are also cumulative, which means that the story begins with one event or one character, and as the story progresses, the events or characters repeat and then build up or add on each time. Many folk songs also use this technique; for example, both "The Farmer in the Dell" and "Old MacDonald Had a Farm" are cumulative songs. (Sing these songs or similar songs or rhymes to give children concrete examples of repetition and accumulation and the difference between them.)

### Reading Focus Question

🔸 As you listen to these folktales, listen for both the cumulative parts and the repetition.

### Post-Reading Questions

🔸 (Return to Focus Question) Discuss examples of accumulation and repetition in the various folktales.

🔸 Most folktales teach a lesson. What lesson did all of these tales teach?

🔸 In most of these tales there was a wise character that pointed out the truth. Who was that character?

🔸 In the folktale from Belgium, the father smacks the little boy, and he, in turn, throws a rock at a bird. When someone has been hurtful toward you, have you ever felt or acted cranky toward someone else?

🔸 Which folktales come from Europe? ("The Hare and the Rumor" from India is quite ancient and is a part of the Jatakas, which is a very old collection of Indian folklore. The tales from Europe are all thought to have derived from the folktale from India. The story from Africa probably developed without any influence from any other culture.)

# Don't Believe Everything You Hear Map

*Directions:* Find the continent for each folktale. Choose a colored pencil or fine-tipped marker to color both the continent and the matching box in the legend.

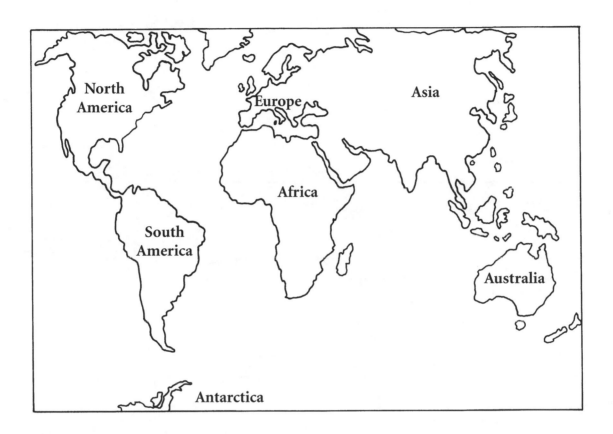

☐ Africa ("Who Can You Believe?")

☐ Belgium ("Mr. Louse and Mrs. Louse")

☐ England ("Chicken Little/Henny Penny")

☐ Germany ("The Day the Sky Fell")

☐ India ("The Hare and the Rumor")

☐ Russia ("The Cock and the Hen")

Copyright © 1999 Linda K. Garrity • *The Tale Spinner*
Fulcrum Publishing • (800) 992-2908 • www.fulcrum-resources.com

# Character Chains

*Directions:* All the folktales in this unit are cumulative, which means the action builds and repeats, finally coming to a quick ending. Cumulative stories are fun, though challenging, to tell. Fill in a name and picture of each animal, then cut out the strips and glue them together in a chain. Now hold up the chain and tell the folktale to your friends.

**Animal:**

**Animal:**

**Animal:**

**Animal:**

**Animal:**

**Animal:**

**Animal:**

# Accordion Book

*Directions:* Choose a variant to tell and illustrate in an accordion book. A partner can create a different variant on the backside of the book. This takes teamwork!

1. Cut eight or more sheets of paper. Any size can be used, but 8" × 11" seems to provide a good space for writing and pictures.

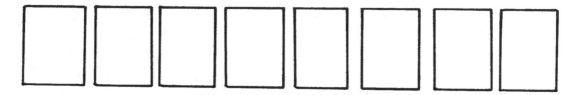

2. Tape the pages together carefully. It is a good idea to tape on both sides.

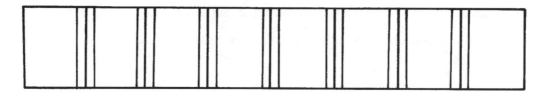

3. Prepare the title pages with the title of the folktale and your name as the author and illustrator in big, neat letters.

4. Write and draw in the words and pictures. It helps to practice on scratch paper first.

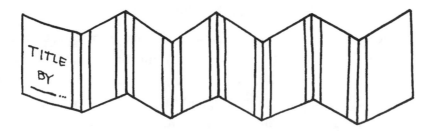

# Bibliography

Butler, Stephen. *Henny Penny*. New York: Tambourine Books, 1991.

Bright, lively illustrations and a surprise ending make this book a good choice.

Galdone, Paul. *Henny Penny*. New York: Clarion Books, 1968.

This small paperback is done in Paul Galdone's inimitable style featuring the large, brightly colored animals with expressive faces. The retelling closely follows the traditional "Henny Penny" cumulative storyline. A solid, basic edition of this folktale, it's sure to please a young audience.

Hobson, Sally. *Chicken Little*. New York: Simon & Schuster, 1994.

Large, richly colored illustrations grace this simple retelling of the original story.

Granowsky, Alvin. *Henny Penny/Brainy Bird Saves the Day*. Austin, Tex.: Steck-Vaughn Company, 1996.

*Henny Penny* is a straightforward version of the original folktale, while *Brainy Bird Saves the Day* is told as a humorous first-person account of the tale by a bird who wants to set the record straight.

Kellogg, Steven. *Chicken Little*. New York: William Morrow, 1985.

After children have heard a traditional version, present this rollicking, updated book by Steven Kellogg. The humorous, finely detailed illustrations combine with the zany storyline to create a delightful tale that is full of new and unexpected twists.

Martin, Rafe. *Foolish Rabbit's Big Mistake*. New York: Putnam, 1985.

In the preface, Rafe Martin explains that this story is from the ancient Indian Jataka tales and is probably the oldest variant of the well known "Henny Penny/Chicken Little" story. With some variation the tale is found in this book on pages 39–40. Ed Young's big, powerful, and brilliantly colored illustrations make this book ideal for story presentation even with quite large groups.

Omerod, Jan. *The Story of Chicken Licken*. New York: Lothrop Lee & Shepard, 1985.

This is an unusual and delightful presentation of the folktale "Chicken Licken." Colorful double spreads show the story unfolding as a school play. Balloon speech from each of the characters tells the story. The audience, shown in black silhouette across the bottom of the page, tells an additional story: parents and children squirm and whisper and a baby escapes from its basket to creep slowly up to the stage and finally join the finale.

Percy, Graham. *Henny-Penny*. New York: Derrydale Books, 1986.

Soft watercolors illustrate this version, which has a happy ending.

Zimmerman, H. Werner. *Henny Penny*. New York: Scholastic Hardcover, 1989.

The colorful, whimsical illustrations have been painted with watercolor on heavy paper. The storyline does not vary from the traditional. The liveliness and humor of the illustrations make this book a delight.

# Chapter 4

# Origin of Thunder

## Introduction

Natural phenomena, especially the weather, have always puzzled and impressed humans. This curiosity has led cultures to create imaginary folktales to explain the wonders of the heavens. The tales presented here highlight one aspect of weather—thunder—and give four creative explanations for this amazing natural occurrence. The folktale from Nigeria features giants, a device used in the folklore of several cultures. If the story generates an interest in giants, the bibliography suggests other readily available folktales that have giants as the main characters. The story from the Lakota tribe is probably the most touching because it has children as the main characters.

### *Quilting*

The "Thunder Quilt" activity is very versatile. You can have each student select a favorite folktale from the four and create a nine-square quilt which highlights all the characters and scenes from the story. This requires a high level of comprehension and accurate sequencing skills.

Or use this as a cooperative-learning activity with each group choosing and creating squares for a single folktale. Elect a chairperson to explain the quilt to the entire class. Children can cut out their squares and tape them together or glue them to large pieces of butcher paper. Square pieces of paper can be used in place of the reproducible.

### *Research and Geography*

The "Climate Zone" and "Climate Clothing" activities teach higher-level thinking skills, geography, and multicultural understanding as children look at the different climatic zones of the globe and the different requirements for clothing and shelter that these climates demand. This activity provides an ideal opportunity to teach children how to use climate maps in atlases—an important skill that is often overlooked. For an extension activity, have children choose the climate they find interesting and research the details of the weather for that climatic zone, the countries in the world that have that climate, and the best clothes and homes for that environment.

Use the "Origin of Thunder Map" to teach the locations of the source countries of these folktales.

### Art

The "Thunder Fold-Up Book" teaches the scientific explanation of thunder in a visual way. To create the booklet, duplicate both sheets. Place the sheet with dotted lines on top of the other one, both facing in the same direction. Fold the pages in half. Then fold them in half in the other direction, making a booklet. Now cut along the dotted lines of the top sheet only to make fold-up flaps that reveal information beneath them. The project may seem a little tricky the first time, but is very appealing to children and helps explain a complicated scientific principle.

### *Research and Storytelling*

Develop a project around the theme of this unit in which children research the answer to a scientific question and also create a folktale explaining the same phenomena. Begin by webbing "I wonder why …" questions on the blackboard. Start with a few questions of your own dealing with major areas of science, then have children add their questions. Group the questions in categories and use this opportunity to teach the names of scientific study areas, such as botany, meteorology, and so on.

Have children select an area of interest and create a new question, or use one already contributed. Use the media center to help students research their questions. Then have them write a paragraph relating their discoveries.

Now switch gears from modern scientific researcher to ancient storyteller. Without science, what imaginative and interesting folktale could be created to answer the same scientific question? When completed, illustrate the two projects and bind them together in a personal book to share with the class.

# Superman vs. the Forest Giant (Africa—Nigeria)

Once there lived a strong man who could not brag enough about his powers. Whenever he brought back wood from the forest, he would boast to his wife, "See all this wood I can carry? Why, I have the strength of ten men; I am truly a superman!"

But his wife would just laugh at his boasting, "Strong you are, oh, yes. But a superman? You would run from a real superman!"

This angered the vain man and he would wander around, muttering to himself, "I *am* a superman. Just show me one man who is stronger than I."

His wife ignored him, gathered her large calabash, placing it on her head, and started down the path to the well. When she arrived, she threw the bucket down into the water, and then began to haul it back up. But alas, the well was deep and the bucket full, and she could not pull it back to the surface. Finally, after much tugging and pulling, she sat down next to the well, thoroughly discouraged.

Soon another woman with a child on her back approached the well to draw water to fill her calabash.

"There is no need to even *try* this well," explained the first woman to the newcomer. "Why, it would take ten men to pull a bucket of water out of this well."

"Do not despair. I will help you," said the second woman.

With that, she untied the tiny child from her back and carried him over to the well. He grasped the rope in his chubby little fingers and easily pulled the bucket to the surface.

"Allah be praised!" exclaimed the first woman. "Your son is so strong! And what is your husband's name?"

"His name is Superman," answered the woman, as she put her child on her back.

When the wife returned home with the calabash of water, she told her husband about the woman at the well with the powerful baby and a husband named Superman. The jealousy in her husband boiled to the surface like bubbles rising in a simmering kettle.

"Take me to this family tomorrow and we will see which of us is truly Superman," said the husband.

"Please forget this foolishness," implored the wife. "With the baby that strong, there is no telling how powerful the father could be!"

But her husband would not listen to her. And so the next morning when she picked up her calabash to go to the well, he went with her. Events happened much as before: the man was not able to draw the bucket out of the well, but when the woman and the baby arrived, the little one was able to lift it with ease. This angered the man and he demanded to follow the woman home to meet her husband.

Both women thought this was very foolhardy, but could not dissuade the man, so he followed the woman home. When they arrived at the woman's compound, she said to the man, "My husband is away hunting right now, so you can hide in this huge water pot until he comes home. Then you can catch a glimpse of him before you decide to meet him."

"I don't need to hide!" exclaimed the man. "I am not afraid of your husband."

"Very well," returned the woman, "but he *did* eat an entire elephant for breakfast today."

At that the man climbed in the water pot and hid until dinnertime. Soon Superman returned from hunting.

"Wife, wife," called Superman, "is my elephant ready to eat?"

Superman ate his hearty meal, cracking the elephant bones like twigs. Meanwhile, the foolish man cowered in the water pot hoping that Superman's hunger was being completely satisfied by the elephant.

Finally, Superman and his wife and baby laid down to sleep. "Wife, I smell the scent of a human being!" said Superman.

"Oh, husband, it is only me that you are smelling," said the wife.

He was doubtful, but eventually fell asleep. His wife then carefully crept out of bed and went over to the water pot where the man was still hiding.

"Are you satisfied now?" whispered the disgusted wife into the deep pot. "Why didn't you believe me when I told you that my husband was a superman?"

"I am truly sorry," said the humble man. "You were right. He is a superman and I am not. Now, how can I escape from here?"

"Wait until you hear him snoring," answered the wife. "Then quietly crawl out of this pot, run as fast as you can, and never come back here again."

Time passed slowly in the night, but after a while the man heard Superman begin to snore. Ever so carefully, he climbed over the rim of the pot, crept to the doorway, and then ran as swiftly as his feet could carry him.

Just as he thought his lungs would burst, he heard the deep voice of Superman coming behind him. "I smell the scent of a human being!" roared Superman.

The frightened man kept on running, even though he was nearly dead from fatigue. Just as he had about given up all hope of ever escaping from Superman, he came upon a clearing and there, just ahead, sat a huge man under a giant baobab tree. The man was calmly eating an elephant and throwing the bones over his shoulder into the forest.

"Halt!" he bellowed. "Why are you running so fast?"

"Because Superman is chasing me," answered the man. "Can you help me?"

"Why, of course," answered the huge man. "I am called the Forest Giant and I am not afraid of anyone!"

They did not have long to wait. Soon Superman came roaring into the clearing.

"Give me back my man!" he demanded. "Though he is only a small snack, I nevertheless intend to eat him."

"Then you will need to come over here to get him," answered the Forest Giant, as he stood up and prepared to fight. With that the two began to tug and wrestle, so the poor man used this opportunity to run all the way back through the forest to his home, never once glancing back at the giant fighters.

When he arrived home, his wife was amazed to see him, thinking that he surely would be killed by Superman.

After the man related all his close calls to his wife, she said, "I hope you have learned your lesson from this. No matter how strong or smart or rich you are, there is always someone who is more so."

"You are *so* right," agreed the man humbly. "I will never forget this."

And as for the Superman and the Forest Giant, they fought so hard that they both rose up into the heavens. Most of the time, they sit on separate clouds and rest. But when you look up into the sky and see it turn dark and rumble, you know that it is not thunder, but merely Superman and Forest Giant, fighting once again.

# Why the Thunder Man Hurls Thunderbolts (Australia—Aborigine)

 Tjambuwal, which means the Thunder Man, was a fearsome giant who long ago dwelled upon the shining beaches of Northern Australia. His torso alone was the size of the eucalyptus tree that grows on the Australian continent. The aboriginal peple have lived in this area, called the Arnhem Land, since the Dreamtime, a time very different from today, when gods and other celestial beings laid down the laws that govern the Aborigines to this day.

Long ago two of Thunder Man's sons were killed. Thunder Man's heart was filled with sorrow; he wailed and shook his fists at the sky and could not be comforted. Finally the gods took pity on Thunder Man and changed his sons' bodies into smooth, white stones that lay scattered upon the beach. This brought Thunder Man much comfort, because now, when he ambled along the beach, he could see his sons and feel their presence near him.

The unending hot, dry weather of the Dreamtime proved a hardship on the animals. The goanna lizards grew parched without rain and the other animals hid in the undergrowth to escape from the endless sun. Thunder Man paced up and down the beach, worrying about the creatures. Suddenly, he bent down, picked up a smooth, white stone and hurled it aloft. The spirit of the stone exploded in the air and became a huge cumulus cloud, billowing into the sky over the bay. When the cloud filled the sky and grew dark, it released its rain. How the plants and animals of Arnhem rejoiced! From that day until present time, Thunder Man throws white stones into the sky at the beginning of each rainy season. The spirits of his beloved sons come down in each raindrop, nourishing the people, animals, and plants that live here below.

Once during the Dreamtime, a Man went fishing with his spear. Luck was with him and he speared many fat white fish for his dinner. Hurrying home to his hut, he quickly built a roaring campfire and skewered the fish on sticks to grill them. Soon the smoke and the tantalizing aroma of the cooking fish wafted upward into the sky. This attracted the attention of Thunder Man, who was floating through the sky on cumulus clouds. When he peered down, he discovered that the man was cooking a type of fish which was denied to common man to catch and eat.

This caused Thunder Man to fill with rage. Finally, he could contain his anger no longer. He struck two massive clubs together, booming his discontent with the man below. This caused the clouds to drop their water, extinguishing the flames in the fire, so the man could not cook and eat the forbidden fish. Finally, Thunder Man came back down to earth to hit the man with his club and kill him.

The People say that kind Tjambuwal gives the earth the rainy season to save it from the sun and the heat. But every once in a while, Tjambuwal shows his angry side and booms out a clap of thunder to remind the people not to eat forbidden foods and to follow the laws of Aborigine society.

# Thunder and Fire
# (United States—California Indian)

n the early days, Thunder kept fire in his lodge at the very top of Lonely Mountain. The lodge had a huge fire pit and a large smoke hole in the top to allow the smoke to rise and blow away. Thunder's four daughters—Clouds, Rain, Ice, and Lightning—slept around the fire pit, keeping guard over this valuable treasure.

Meanwhile, all the animals suffered. They had no fire pits in their lodges to keep them warm at night. They could not cook their food and had to eat game raw, wasting many of the tougher pieces that were too difficult to eat without being cooked.

At last the Season of Colorful Leaves began to fade, and all knew that soon the Season of Cold Nights would begin. The animals called a council.

"I am tired of eating only raw meat," said Wolf. "It would be so fine to see meat roasting on a spit over a hot fire in front of my lodge."

"Yes, and with the Season of Cold Nights soon pinching our toes, it would be good to sleep around a warm fire pit," said Grizzly Bear.

The animals' gazes looked upward to Lonely Mountain where they could see a thin trail of smoke wafting through the sky from the smoke hole of Thunder's high lodge.

"But how can we take fire away from Thunder?" asked Rabbit. "Thunder is strong and powerful, and we are weak."

"Yes, and Lonely Mountain is very high, with steep cliffs," added Coyote.

The council would have ended on this note if Eagle had not stepped into their midst.

"Thunder is strong, true, but he is also wicked," said Eagle. "If we are brave and clever, we can outwit him and bring fire to all the animals."

So the animals chose Mouse, Dog, Deer, and Coyote to make the journey to Lonely Mountain. It was a difficult journey, but the animals helped one another and eventually they made it to the crest of Lonely Mountain.

Mouse scurried up the side of Thunder's lodge to peer down into the smoke hole and survey the situation inside. Fortunately, Thunder was gone, but his four daughters were sleeping around the fire pit, which had burned down to hot coals. So Mouse quietly climbed down the center pole in the lodge and crept over to the fire. He wrapped three coals in green leaves and left the lodge without disturbing any of Thunder's daughters.

The animals decided to divide up the coals and escape through different routes to increase their chances of at least one of them making it back to their village. One coal was placed in Dog's ear and he took off. Coyote took a coal between his teeth and dashed away. Mouse kept the last coal and rode away on swift Deer's back.

The animals hurried as quickly as they could and all seemed well—at least for a time. They had returned to the base of Lonely Mountain and could see their village a short distance ahead, when they heard the familiar rumble and roar of Thunder, who had by now returned to his lodge and discovered the theft of fire.

"Wake up!" he raged at his daughters. "Someone has stolen fire while you four slept!"

"Hurry!" he continued. "We must find the thieves and deal with them."

The villagers shuddered as they looked up into the sky to see dark Clouds, Rain, Ice, and Lightning coming down from the top of Lonely Mountain toward them. But overpowering everything was the boom of violent Thunder.

The animals with the coals began to run faster than ever, but, alas, their true nature betrayed them. Coyote, in his fear, dropped his coal, and Rain, who was close on his heels, snatched it up. Then Dog laughed at Coyote for dropping his coal. As Dog laughed, he shook his head, and his coal fell from his ear, where it was picked up by Clouds. That left only Mouse, riding on Deer's back, with a coal for the village.

"Oh, my little friend," gasped Deer. "I can run no further! Pass your coal on to an animal who has not been running."

So Mouse passed the coal on to Tree Squirrel, who led Thunder and his daughters on a wild chase up and down trees until she, too, was weary. She passed the coal on to Frog, who could leap so swiftly that Thunder could not catch him. Hail kept up the pursuit and grabbed Frog with her icy fingers, breaking off his tail. Because of this, Frogs have never had tails since that time. Meanwhile the coal flew out of Frog's front legs into a hollow stump at the edge of the pond.

"Aha!" roared Thunder triumphantly. "The fire is mine once again!"

Just as Thunder swooped down to retrieve the coal, out popped Skunk, who lived in the hollow stump and feared no one.

"How dare you come to earth to harass the animals!" fumed Skunk, and with that, he shot his special arrow into Thunder.

Thunder had finally met his match. His daughters carried him back to the top of Lonely Mountain, where he soon recovered. Though his voice is often heard booming from his lodge high on Lonely Mountain, he has never again come down to earth to bother the animals.

His daughters still live with him in his lodge, but all come down to earth from time to time, sometimes together and sometimes separately, because they are still angry that they were outsmarted by the animals.

Meanwhile all the animals have enjoyed the benefits of fire from that day forward.

# The Lodge of the Bear
## (United States—Lakota Indian)

ong ago a band of Lakotas camped near the Black Hills, the Paha-sapa. Among them were a young boy and his sister, children of one of the wise men of the band. Once day the boy and girl went out to pick berries. They wandered on and on, never realizing how far they were from home.

Suddenly they heard a deep growl behind them. Turning, they saw a huge bear and to their dismay they also saw that not a tipi was in sight. They were all alone on the prairie.

As they had no weapons, they decided that the only thing for them to do was run. When the bear saw them run, he started after them, growling more fiercely than before.

The poor children, terrified, ran as they had never run before, but despite all their efforts the bear gained on them steadily. Realizing there was no escape, they stopped and turned toward their pursuer. If they were to die, then they would die like brave warriors, facing their enemy.

When the bear saw them stop, he too stopped. Standing up on his hind legs he glowered at them.

While they stood like that, the little girl said to her brother: Brother, let us call upon Wakan-tanka, the Great Mystery. Surely He will help us. So the two of them, still facing the big bear, raised their arms to the sky and called to Wakan-tanka to help them.

A strange thing happened. The ground on which they stood began to rise, and by the time the astonished bear decided to charge, the two children were safe on top of a tall butte.

The bear was so angry, he tried again and again to climb the steep sides of the place where the children had found refuge. He would back away, then running swiftly, he would jump up and try to reach the mountaintop. But each time he missed and as he went sliding back to the bottom, his big sharp claws made the scratches you see running up and down the sides. He persevered until he had clawed his way completely around the sides and then he stopped because he was exhausted. In fact he was so tired that he couldn't move and he died of starvation and thirst at the foot of the butte.

The boy and girl lived all their lives on the butte and after they died, their spirits were often seen by people passing that way. Some might think it is only a few fleecy white clouds, but wise ones know it is the children playing and dancing. In the summer when the thunder rolls, people say it is Bear growling.

# Discussion Questions

### Prereading Questions

▨ These four folktales are a type of folk literature called "*pourquoi*," (por *kwaw*) which is a French word meaning "why." In ancient times before the development of science, people wondered about the world around them. Because they had no scientific answers to explain nature, they created stories to explain the wonders of their world. Each of these tales is very different from one another, though they all try to explain why we have thunder.

▨ Why do you think so many cultures would have thought it was important to try to explain thunder to their people?

▨ Why do you think all the stories would be so different?

▨ What do you feel when you hear thunder? What safety measures should you take?

### Reading Focus Question

▨ As you listen to these stories, think of why it would be important to know the actual cause of thunder.

### Post-Reading Questions

▨ (Return to Focus Question) Why is it good to know the cause of thunder?

▨ When you first heard the word "Superman" in the folktale from Africa, what did it bring to your mind? How was it used in this story? Some cultures feature giants in their folklore and other cultures never do. Do you know some cultures that have giants in their folktales? Do you know any other imaginary creatures in folktales?

▨ In the folktale from Nigeria the woman says, "Allah be praised." What does that tell you about the culture of this folktale?

▨ Often a single *pourquoi* tale will explain more than one fact in nature. What other aspects of weather are explained in the Lakota Indian tale?

▨ What two facts of nature are explained in the Aborigine tale?

▨ The California Indian tale explains both why Thunder now stays up in the sky and also how the animals stole fire. What other nature facts are explained in this tale?

## Origin of Thunder Map

*Directions:* Find the continent for each folktale. Choose a colored pencil or fine-tipped marker to color both the continent and the matching box in the legend.

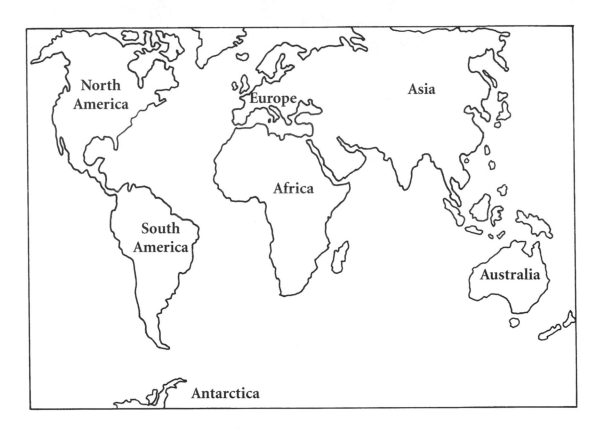

☐ Africa–Nigeria ("Superman vs. the Forest Giant")

☐ Australia–Aborigine ("Why the Thunder Man Hurls Thunderbolts")

☐ United States–California Indian ("Thunder and Fire")

☐ United States–Lakota Indian ("The Lodge of the Bear")

Copyright © 1999 Linda K. Garrity • *The Tale Spinner*
Fulcrum Publishing • (800) 992-2908 • www.fulcrum-resources.com

## Thunder Quilt

*Directions:* Either color the square below or trace the square onto colored paper. Choose a variant from the "Origin of Thunder" unit. Write the name of the culture and draw in an object or character from that story. Then cut out your quilt square. It can be taped to other squares from the same variant made by other children to make a large quilt.

**Culture:**

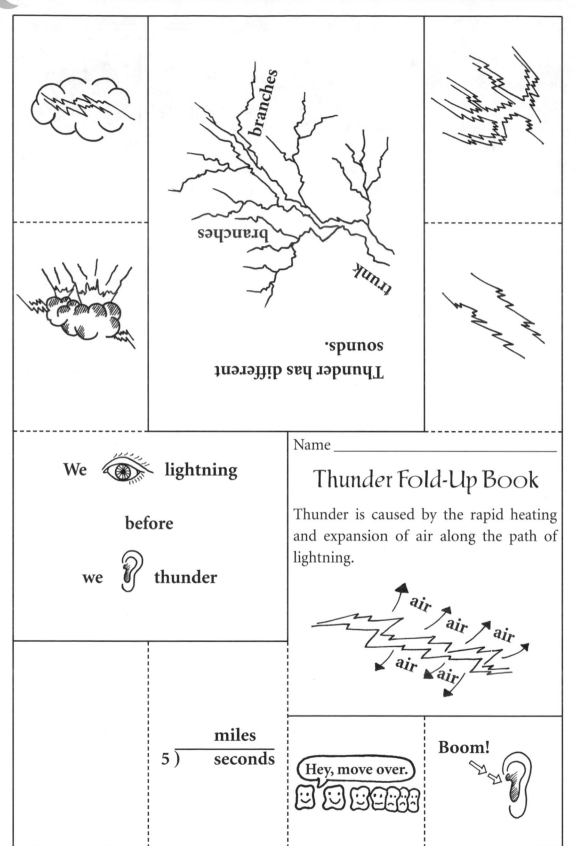

**Thunder has different sounds.**

branches

branches

trunk

We 👁 lightning

before

we 👂 thunder

$5{\overline{)\,\dfrac{\text{miles}}{\text{seconds}}}}$

Name_____

## Thunder Fold-Up Book

Thunder is caused by the rapid heating and expansion of air along the path of lightning.

Hey, move over.

Boom!

continued

You cannot see
lightning strike
the inside of a
cloud, but you
can hear the
thunder.

Branches of
lightning
cause a sharp,
crackling
sound.

Thunder from
far away makes
a long, deep
rumbling
sound.

The main
trunk of
lightning
causes a loud
boom or
explosion.

**Light travels
faster than
sound.**

**Count the number
of seconds
between seeing
lightning and
hearing thunder
and then divide by
five. That will tell
you how many
miles you are from
the lightning
strike.**

**Air particles
crowd together
to form a
sound wave.**

**The sound
wave reaches
the human ear
as a roar or
explosion.**

Fulcrum Publishing • (800) 992-2908 • www.fulcrum-resources.com

# Climate Zone

*Directions:* Look up the following countries or states to find out their climates: Northern Australia, Northern Canada or Alaska (state), or New Zealand, Nigeria, United States. Then color in the legend and the location of the countries on their continents.

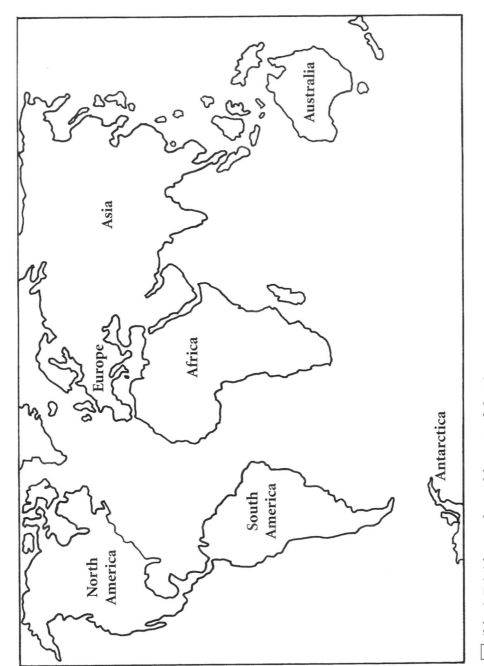

- ☐ (blue) Frigid or polar-cold most of the time
- ☐ (green) Temperate or continental-hot summer and cold winter
- ☐ (yellow) Subtropical-warm and either dry or rainy
- ☐ (red) Tropical-hot and rainy most of the time

# Climate Clothing

*Directions:* The average, long-range weather is called climate. Climate effects the types of clothing people wear. The folktales from the origins of thunder and fire units come from a wide variety of climates. Children from those cultures are pictured here wearing their traditional clothing. Study the climate map on the previous page. Write in the climate for each child. Then color each child's clothing.

_____   _____   _____

_____   _____

# Bibliography

Calhoun, Mary. *Big Sixteen*. New York: William Morrow, 1983.

From the Old South comes this tale of a black folk hero from slavery times whose name, Big Sixteen, refers to his shoe size. Trina Schart Hyman's excellent illustrations complement this unlikely story of a giant.

Cauley, Lorinda Bryan. *Jack and the Beanstalk*. New York: Putnam, 1983.

Cauley's vibrant illustrations create a fine version of the old English folktale with the giant. (Some versions of this tale feature an ogre, rather than a giant.)

dePaola, Tomie. *Fin M'Coul, the Giant of Knockmany Hill*. New York: Holiday House, 1981.

The storytelling and artistic talents of dePaola combine to create this delightful Irish folktale of the final battle between two legendary giants, Fin M'Coul and Cucullin.

———. *The Mysterious Giant of Barletta*. New York: Harcourt Brace Jovanovich, 1984.

Here dePaola's talents are used to tell the myth of the giant statue in Barletta, Italy.

De Regniers, Beatrice Schenk. *Jack the Giant-Killer*. New York: Atheneum, 1987.

Told in whimsical verse, this book has a final section with tips on how to deal with giants.

DeSpain, Pleasant. *Strongheart Jack and the Beanstalk*. Little Rock, Ark.: August House Publishers, 1995.

Retold from an original source, this version expands on the familiar story and tells more about Jack's background and more about the giants.

Kellogg, Steven. *Paul Bunyan*. New York: William Morrow, 1984.

One can always look to the rollicking American tall tales for a story about a giant. Kellogg's story of Paul Bunyan and his blue ox, Babe, fill the bill in the giant department.

Pearson, Susan. *Jack and the Beanstalk.* New York: Simon & Schuster, 1989.

This beautiful version depicts a giant who is also an ogre.

Walker, Paul Robert. *Big Men, Big Country: A Collection of American Tall Tales.* New York: Harcourt Brace, 1993.

This fine collection features the larger-than-life American tall tale characters.

Walker, Paul Robert. *Giants! Stories from Around the World.* New York: Harcourt Brace, 1995.

*Giants!* is a gem with seven folktales from different cultures around the world.

# Chapter 5

# Origin of Fire

## Introduction

Introduce this unit by having children speculate on the quality of life for ancient people before they discovered how to create sparks for fire. Then explore the possibilities and advantages this skill provided for these people. It is no wonder that the creation of fire filled people with awe and respect for its power. What techniques for creating fire did they discover other than fires started by lightning? Note that two of the three folktales conclude with the belief that fire lies within wood and knowledge allowed people to bring it forth.

The Polynesian variant "Maui and the Secret of Fire" originated with Maori people from New Zealand and then spread throughout the Polynesian Islands. This tale is identified as Hawaiian because it is also told there, but it probably came to those islands by other Polynesians traveling over the Pacific Ocean in boats.

The California Indian tale "Thunder and Fire" found on pages 53–55 in the preceding unit is a fitting folktale for this unit as well.

### Geography

Use the "Origin of Fire Map" activity to teach children where to locate the source countries or states for these folktales.

### Science

"Three Conditions for Fire" is a science activity that teaches what conditions must be present for fire to exist. The picture for oxygen could be a cloud or the scientific designation, $O_2$. The kindling temperature can be represented by a thermometer.

## Comprehension

"Fire Photo Album" requires a high level of comprehension and sequencing to remember all the main events in the story and then illustrate them. An extension could involve oral storytelling to younger children with the storyteller using the album as a prop.

## Research

Forest fires are a natural phenomena, yet there is controversy over the value of allowing forest fires in our National Forests to burn. With the help of the librarian, have boys and girls research this controversy using periodical resources. Form panel discussions to argue pros and cons. Bring the activity to life by having someone from the National Forest Service speak to the class on this topic.

Fire gives us both heat and light. Ask your class which commodity they consider the most important. Why?

Methods of lighting and heating have an interesting history. Discovering the innovations in both these areas would make a fascinating research project. Make it a cooperative-learning project, with each member of the group assigned to illustrate and explain an historical device used to heat or light a home.

# How the People Got Fire
## (United States—Cherokee Indian)

In the beginning there was no fire. The whole world was cold, until the thunders of the sky struck an old sycamore tree with lightning and put fire in the bottom of it.

Nobody could get it, however, because the tree was on an island, and the fire was inside the tree. Everyone could see the smoke coming out of the old hollow tree, but nobody knew how to get it.

Every animal and bird who knew how to swim or fly offered to go.

They sent Raven first because he was big and strong. He flew across the water and lighted in the top of the tree. He sat there wondering what to do next, and the heat scorched his feathers black. So he flew home. This is why Raven is black today.

Little Wahuhu, the screech owl, went next. He flew across the water to the island and looked down into the hollow tree to see the fire. A blast of hot air puffed up and nearly burned out his eyes. So he had to give up. His eyes are still red today and he can still hardly see in the daytime.

Hoot Owl and Horned Owl went next. The fire was burning hotter and hotter all the time. When they looked down into the tree, the smoke blinded them and the flying ashes made white rings around their eyes. The white rings are still there.

Then little Black-racer Snake said he would go. He swam through the water fast. When he got to the island, he sped through the grass to the foot of the tree. He went into the tree through a small hole in the bottom, but it was so hot in there he had to come out. He was scorched blacker than ever.

Big Blacksnake went next. His name was Climber because he always climbed up the outside of a tree, just as blacksnakes do today. When he poked his head down the tree to investigate the fire, the smoke choked him, and he fell in. It was awful! He climbed out again all right, but he was burned black all over. He too had to go back without fire.

So the birds and the animals and the snakes held a big council. Who would go for fire? Who would know how to get it? Nobody was very eager to go any more.

Finally, Water Spider said she would go. This was not the little water spider that skitters around on top of the water, but the big one with the handsome, black, hairy coat with red stripes. She is very famous. She can run on top of the water and she can dive to the bottom.

"I'll go," she said.

"You can get there, all right," the wise ones answered her, "but how can you carry fire?"

"I know how," she said.

So WaterSpider sat down and spun a strong thread. She wove it into a *tusti* (which means bowl), and this she fastened onto her back. Then off she went.

She ran across the top of the water. When she came to the tree, the fire was still burning but beginning to die down. She put one little coal of fire in the tusti bowl and ran back across the water with the tusti on her back.

Everybody was waiting; everybody was watching. They could see a tiny feather of smoke rising from the tusti.

This is how people first received fire, and mankind has used it and kept warm ever since. Water Spider still carries her little tusti bowl today.

# How Fire and Water Came to the Far North (United States–Eskimo)

 long time ago there was no water and no fire in the Land of the Far North. When the days were long and sunny, the People were happy. They could lick the dew that clung to the leaves and grass. They could eat berries, roots, and the eggs of birds. But when the days and nights were dark and cold, as they so often were, they were miserable.

Now it so happened that a man and his son lived together in the lodge that had been their family's since the man's father before him and his father before him and his father before him. And always, in one corner of this barren and humble lodge, had stood two magnificently carved chests. They were both fashioned of a rich wood, and completely covered with ornate carvings of plants, animals, and flowers of the Land of the Far North. The only difference between the two chests was the designs on the covers. One had a carving of a bright sun shining upon the earth. The other one had a carving of a stream winding around and around the cover of the chest.

The man told his son, "These two chests have been here in this lodge as long as our people have lived here. We must never open them for we do not know what we would unleash into the world."

"Yes, father," answered the son obediently, though he often stroked the wood with his fingers and wondered what spirits resided within the chests.

Watching over the chests was a great burden for this little family. When the father left the lodge to hunt, the son stayed behind to guard the chests. When the son went out to play, the father had to stay inside the lodge. The boy never had enough time to make a good friend and gradually he lost interest in going out at all.

Then one day a strange hunter happened by their lodge and asked for shelter from the weather. The son welcomed the man inside, as such was the custom of hospitality in the Land of the Far North, but he felt uneasy because his father was away hunting.

The hunter had not rested very long in the lodge before his eyes fell upon the chests in the corner.

"What beautiful chests!" admired the man. "They also look very old."

"Yes, they have belonged to our family for many generations," agreed the boy proudly.

"These carvings are splendid," continued the man. "Could you tell me the stories behind them?"

"I do not know the stories," said the boy softly.

"But why not?" asked the man. "Surely if these chests have been in your family for generations, you know the stories! I am weary from my travels and would enjoy hearing some tales."

The boy felt embarrassed because he appeared unfriendly to the stranger. So he decided to explain the unusual situation to the man so he would not think him ill-mannered.

"These are secret chests," he began. "No one in my family has ever opened them, because they have evil spirits inside that could cause great harm if unleashed into the world. So each generation of my family guards against this, and we don't talk about the chests. That way we aren't tempted to open them ourselves."

The boy felt that this explanation would satisfy the hunter and encourage him to speak no more of the chests. But it was not to be. The explanation only increased the man's curiosity.

"Why is your family so certain that there are only evil spirits within the chests? What if there are kind spirits inside that could help the People?" asked the man.

"I don't know," admitted the boy, and he stood up and paced around the lodge nervously because he was upset with the stranger and his questions and wished his father would return to take care of the situation.

The hunter sensed the boy's discomfort and changed the subject to talk of other matters. But his curiosity was still aroused and so finally he said to the boy, "Why don't you go outside to see if your father is coming back from the hunt? I have some questions for him before I go on my way."

"Very well, my father should be back soon!" agreed the boy eagerly as he scurried out the door of the lodge.

As soon as the boy was standing on the hillock outside the lodge, the stranger strode over and quickly opened the chest with the winding stream on the cover. As the cover slowly opened, there was a stirring inside the chest. Suddenly clear, fresh water spurted from the box like a drinking fountain and ran out the front door of the lodge, forming a small brook. It then flowed across the meadow to a lower area, becoming a river.

As the boy turned and noticed all the water coming from his lodge, he ran back inside.

"What has happened? Where is the water coming from?" he started to say as he saw the opened chest and the relentless stream of water pouring out of it.

"Yes! Isn't this amazing?" exclaimed the hunter. "A blessing for the People!"

And then, before the boy could protest, the man opened the lid of the second chest. A bright glow came from the box that seemed to grow and illuminate the earth. Finally, heat from the glow became intense and flashed into flames which raced across the meadow and into the forest. As it touched each tree, its magic illuminated the tree without destroying it and then it danced on to the next tree.

Since that day, all the People have enjoyed fresh water in the streams, rivers, and lakes, and fire to brighten and warm their lodges and cook their food. They also know that within each tree lies the magic of fire and with patience it can be brought to life.

# Maui and the Secret of Fire (United States—Hawaiian or Maori)

In the early days, man did not know how to make fire. Maui, who was always curious, and sometimes mischievous, decided to get this knowledge. Fire, of course, comes from the underworld beneath the surface of the land. The Goddess of Fire, Mahu Ika (*mow* hoo *ee* kuh), stands guard over it. Maui found a deep hole in the earth and followed it down to the underworld.

"Mahu Ika, with all respect," began Maui, "the people need fire. Could you help us with this request?"

"Yes, I will give you one of my flaming fingernails to take back with you," said the goddess, as she broke off a bit of flaming nail and handed it to Maui.

At first Maui was pleased that this task had been so easy. But as he walked back to his village he realized that although he had fire, he didn't have the secret of how to make it. So Maui buried the fire in water and returned to the underworld.

"Mahu Ika, the fire went out before I could take it to the people. May I have another of your burning fingernails?" asked Maui politely.

Now the goddess knew that Maui was lying, but she decided to go along with his request to discover what the mischievous one was planning. Again Maui buried the flame in either dirt or water. Again he returned to the underworld to ask the goddess for another fingernail.

At last Maui returned to ask for the tenth, and last, fingernail. Mahu Ika had had enough of Maui's mischief. She flew into a rage and chased him out of the underworld. Maui was very swift and the goddess could not catch him. When Maui saw that the goddess was being left behind, he could not resist turning around and taunting her.

"How can the Goddess of all the Underworld be as slow as the turtles in the sand?" teased Maui.

This so enraged Mahu Ika that she stopped and broke off her last burning fingernail and threw it onto some grass growing on the earth. Immediately the grass and then the forests caught fire. Soon the whole earth looked about to be engulfed in flames.

By now even Maui was afraid. He realized that the worlds only hope lie with the God of Wind and Rain, Tawhiri (tah *he* ree).

"Oh powerful Tawhiri, have mercy on your people!" cried Maui to the god in the sky. "Send your rains to save the world!"

The rains began to fall, extinguishing all the flames. Not surprisingly, the Goddess of Fire, seeing her old enemy, rain, fall everywhere, quickly began to retreat to her home in the underworld. Just as she was about to depart from the surface of the earth, however, she realized that the rain would take all fire away from the people. So she stopped long enough to pick up bits of fire and hide them in the souls of trees.

So today the secret of fire remains in the souls of trees where Mahu Ika hid it so long ago. But people know how to bring it out of hiding simply by rubbing one kind of wood against another.

# Discussion Questions

### Prereading Questions

※ These folktales are also called *pourquoi* tales. The previous unit explained what a *pourquoi* tale is. Can you remember what it means?

### Reading Focus Question

※ These folktales all begin with the creatures on earth suffering because of a lack of something. As you listen to the folktales, think both of what was missing and how it changed life for the people and animals on earth when they acquired it.

### Post-Reading Questions

※ (Return to Focus Question) What was missing? How did fire change life when people and animals had it?

※ In the Cherokee, Eskimo, and Hawaiian/Maori tales, fire finally remained on earth in a special form. What was it? In some respects, fire living in wood is a scientific fact. Boy and Girl Scouts usually learn how to create fire from wood. How do they do this? Is it difficult?

※ Like the folktales in the "Origin of Thunder" unit, these stories also explain other facts about nature. What are they?

※ The Cherokee story teaches another lesson as well. What do you think that lesson is?

※ Folklore from various cultures differs in the types of settings. Why? It also differs in the kinds of characters. What kinds of characters are used in the folktales in this unit? The tale from Polynesia is the only one in the book to have gods and goddesses as characters. What other culture (not represented in this book) uses gods and goddesses as characters in folklore?

# Origin of Fire Map

*Directions:* Find the continent for each folktale. Choose a colored pencil or fine-tipped marker to color both the continent and the matching box in the legend.

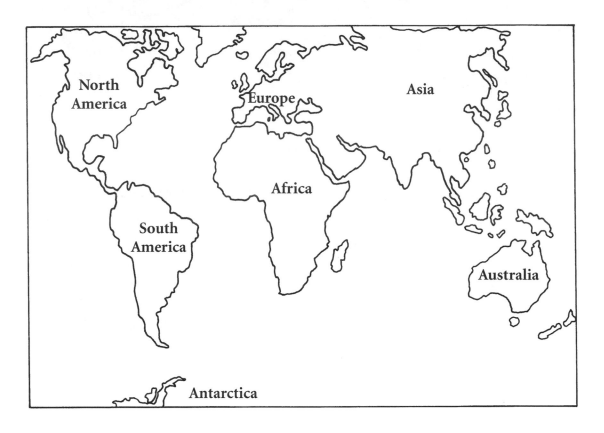

North America

Europe

Asia

Africa

South America

Australia

Antarctica

☐ United States–Cherokee Indian ("How the People Got Fire")

☐ United States–Eskimo ("How Fire and Water Came to the Far North")

☐ United States–Hawaiian or Maori ("Maui and the Secret of Fire")

# Three Conditions for Fire

Three conditions must be present for fire to exist. First there must be a fuel, such as paper or wood. Next there must be oxygen. Last the fuel has to reach a certain temperature, called a kindling temperature, before it can ignite.

*Directions:* Create a wheel showing the three conditions for fire. Draw a picture in each of the three circles on the first page. Then cut out the triangle and small circle on the second page plus the large circle on the first page. Place the triangle on top of the circle and connect the two with a brad.

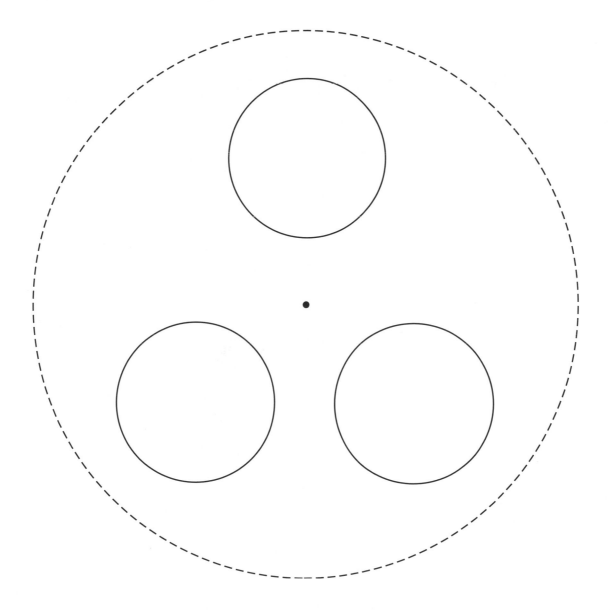

continued

## Three Conditions for Fire (continued)

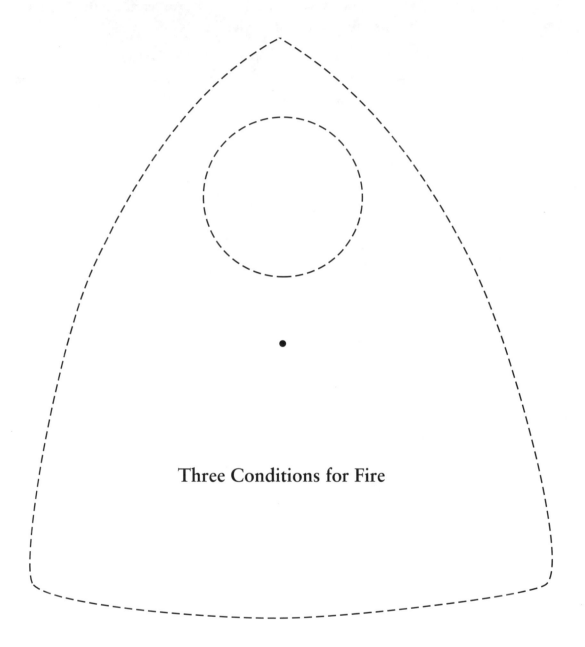

**Three Conditions for Fire**

# Fire Photo Album

*Directions:* Create a photo album for one of the folktale variants on the origin of fire. Color the cover to look like leather, cut it out, and glue it to heavy paper. Trace the cover onto heavy paper to make a back. Start with pictures of the earliest events of the story and end with the final event. Bind the album together with string or yarn.

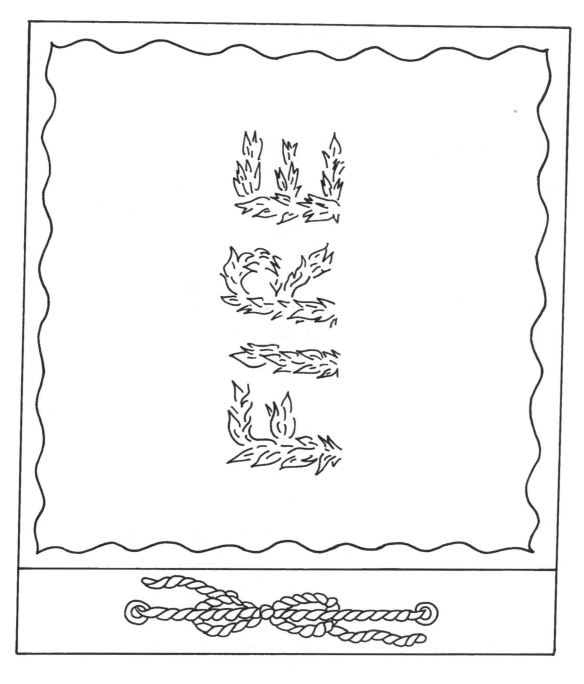

continued

# Fire Photo Album (continued)

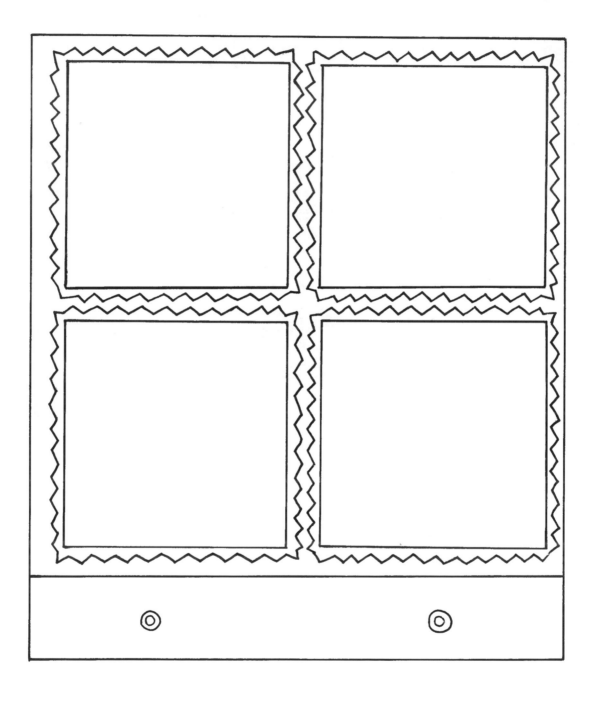

Fulcrum Publishing • (800) 992-2908 • www.fulcrum-resources.com

# Chapter 6

# Spinning Tales

## Introduction

The four folktales featured in this unit—"Rumpelstiltskin," "Tom Tit Tot," "Eileen and the Three Hags," and "Duffy and the Devil"—are all spinning tales which highlight an important concept in folk literature: the use of the number three. There may be three characters, three wishes, three challenges, or events occurring three times. It is interesting that this concept of threeness seems to stay in children's minds whenever they hear or read folktales.

A variant of "Rumpelstiltskin" is included in this unit. The Irish tale "Eileen and the Three Hags" is rare and therefore is included in this unit for your convenience. "Tom Tit Tot" can be found in most collections of English folk or fairy tales. The only version of "Duffy and and the Devil" is the one by Harve and Margot Zemach (see the Bibliography).

"Rumpelstiltskin" is a German folktale collected and published by the Brothers Grimm. It traveled to England in a very similar form, as found in "Tom Tit Tot." The basic folktale is serious; in fact, it is downright tense. But when the Cornish and Irish people began retelling this tale, it became droll; tension was replaced with irony. The Irish and Cornish storytellers wanted their spinning tales to entertain their audience. The lesson learned from their stories is not necessarily "a high moral road." The English and German storytellers kept their listeners on the edge of their seats and taught them a lesson as well.

### Geography

Three of these tales came from the British Isles. Use a globe or large map to help children find England, Ireland, Scotland, Wales, and Cornwall. So many unique cultures within a small geographic area! Use the "Spinning Tales" activity map to reinforce what they've learned. Further research would uncover many interesting facts about these cultures: How are they different? How are they alike? What languages are spoken by each? What special foods are enjoyed in each region? How are they governed?

### Art

The "Spinning Wheel" activity is a simple one made appealing by the brad and the movable wheel. The girl could be the character in any of the four stories. Write the title of the folktale under the drawing on the lower left side. The cut-out figures can be used to decorate the border of a bulletin board featuring projects from this unit.

The "Special 'Three' Ball" highlights the number three concept mentioned earlier. Many simple nursery tales, such as the "The Three Pigs" or "The Three Billy Goats Gruff" are good examples. For younger children one page will probably be plenty; for older ones, one page for each story would be appropriate. Glue or paste works well on the flaps, but staples are quicker and cleaner.

Rumpelstiltskin, Tom Tit Tot, the devil, and the old hags are imaginary characters. What do children think they look like? Collect as many versions of these tales as you can and compare each artist's rendition. Provide clay and, if possible, paint so each child can create a ceramic model of one of the characters.

### Art and Comprehension

The "Spinning Tales" activity is more challenging for children than it appears. They need to create a "snapshot" for each scene in the folktale. The photo album, when completed correctly, demonstrates a high level of comprehension and sequencing.

### Research

"Make-Believe Research" is a fascinating research project for older children. The provided list of magical characters to research is comprehensive, though there are surely other characters yet to be discovered. The culture that seems to have the most magical characters in its folk literature is Irish.

Tom Tit Tot and Rumpelstiltskin are odd names. Most names have an origin and a special meaning. The media center should have books on names or you may know someone who has an inexpensive baby-naming book you can borrow. Have each child look up their first or middle name to discover the meaning (or in the case of unusual names, how or why the parent created the name). Create tag board name plates with the name drawn in pencil and traced over with glitter, and the meaning written neatly in pen beneath. Decorate the classroom with them and later give them to the children to keep.

# Rumpelstiltskin (Germany)

nce upon a time there was a poor miller who had a beautiful daughter. Now it happened that on his way to the village, the miller encountered the king. Wanting to appear important in the presence of the king, the miller said, "I have a daughter who can spin straw into gold."

"Marvelous," replied the greedy king. "Bring her to the palace tomorrow and I will see if she is as clever as you say."

"Very well, sire," replied the poor miller, regretting his boast.

When the miller's daughter was brought to the palace the next day, the king immediately escorted her to a room which was filled with straw.

He gave the girl a spinning wheel and empty spools, and said, "Now start to work and spin all the straw in this room into gold by morning. If you fail, you will die."

At that, the king locked the door and left the girl inside the room all alone.

The poor miller's daughter sat beside the spinning wheel looking at all the straw piled high in the room until she began to weep.

Suddenly the door opened and in stepped a tiny man. "Mistress Miller," said he, "why do you weep?"

"I must spin all this straw into gold," cried the poor girl, "or I will die!"

"What will you give me if I do it for you?" asked the little man.

"My necklace," replied the girl.

The little man took the necklace, sat down beside the spinning wheel and started to work. Whir, whir, whir went the wheel, quickly spinning the dry straw into shining spools of gold. And so it went until every piece of straw had been spun into gold.

As soon as the first rays of daylight touched the palace roof, the king walked into the room. He was amazed and delighted by what he saw. The sight of all that gleaming gold made him greedier than ever. So he had the girl taken to an even larger room filled with straw and ordered her to spin it into gold or die.

Left alone, the miller's daughter began to weep.

As before, the door opened and in stepped the tiny man. "Mistress Miller," said he, "why do you weep?"

"I must spin all this straw into gold," cried the poor girl, "or I will die!"

"What will you give me if I do it for you?" asked the little man.

"My ring," replied the girl.

The little man took the ring, sat down beside the spinning wheel and started to work. Whir, whir, whir went the wheel, quickly spinning the dry straw into shining spools of gold. And so it went until every piece of straw had been spun into gold.

As soon as the first rays of daylight touched the palace roof, the king walked into the room. Again he was amazed and delighted by what he saw. Instead of being satisfied, he became even more greedy at the sight of all that gleaming gold.

Then he thought, "I could not find a richer wife in all the world."

So he had the girl taken to an even larger room filled with straw and said, "Spin all this straw into gold by morning and you shall become my wife. If you don't, you will die."

Left alone, the miller's daughter began to weep.

As before, the door opened and in stepped the tiny man. "Mistress Miller," said he, "why do you weep?"

"I must spin all this straw into gold," cried the poor girl, "or I will die!"

"What will you give me if I do it for you?" asked the little man.

"I have nothing else to give you," replied the girl.

"Then promise me when you become queen, you will give me your first-born child," said the little man.

At first the girl gasped. But then she thought, "Who knows what will happen? And besides, I have no other choices to save myself."

When the miller's daughter promised what he had asked, the little man sat down beside the spinning wheel and started to work. Whir, whir, whir went the wheel, quickly spinning the dry straw into shining spools of gold. And so it went until every piece of straw had been spun into gold.

When the king walked in the room at dawn and found everything as he had ordered, he immediately made arrangements for a royal wedding. The beautiful miller's daughter became a queen and forgot all about the little man.

When a year had passed, the queen gave birth to a beautiful baby. One day the little man appeared in her room and said, "Now you must give me what you promised. I have come for the child."

The queen was greatly distraught and offered the little man all the riches in the kingdom if only he would let her keep her precious baby.

But the little man only replied, "All the treasures in the kingdom are not as dear to me as a living creature."

The queen cried so piteously that at last the little man was moved.

"I will give you three days to guess my name," he said. "If by that time you know it, you may keep your child."

All day long the queen did nothing but think of names.

When the little man returned that evening, she began with, "Caspar, Melchior, and Balthazar," and continued on with every name she knew.

To each name the little man replied, "That is not my name."

On the second day the queen sent her most trusted servant to all the homes in the nearby villages to learn of new and unusual names.

When the little man returned that evening, she began with, "Crookshanks, Spindleshanks, and Muttonchop," and continued on with every name she knew.

To each name the little man replied, "That is not my name."

On the third day the queen sent her most trusted servant to all the homes in the countryside to learn of new and unusual names.

When the servant returned that day, she said, " I had not been able to find any new names, but as I came upon a hidden place in the deepest part of the forest, I saw a strange little man dancing around a fire and singing:

> Today I brew, tomorrow I bake,
> After that, the baby I'll take.
> The queen will never know my game
> For Rumpelstiltskin is my name!"

Soon afterward the little man appeared in the queen's chambers.

"You have three more guesses and then I take the baby," said the little man.

"Is your name William?" asked the queen.

"That is not my name."

"Is your name Thomas?"

"That is not my name."

"Is your name … Rumpelstiltskin?"

"Who told you? Who told you?" shrieked Rumpelstiltskin as he jumped up and down in a fury.

Rumpelstiltskin stamped up and down so hard that he disappeared. And he was never seen again.

# Eileen and the Three Hags (Ireland)

Once there was a poor widow woman living up Donegal way with a daughter who was as lazy and shiftless as the day is long. At long last the widow grew so disgusted with the girl's idle ways, that she grabbed a skillet and began chasing the girl about the hut, screaming and yelling and whacking the girl.

Now it just so happened that the king's son was out riding nearby when he heard the terrible clamor coming from within the shabby hut. He and his men quickly rode over to the hut, drawing rein just outside the door.

"Good lady, what ever is the matter?" called out the prince.

The widow scurried to the door and quickly curtsied when she saw it was a noble-man and his men.

"Oh, sire, it's a terrible problem I have with me daughter, Eileen. Such a hard worker she is, that I can't get her to stop and take a rest," explained the widow, not want-ing the prince to know the truth about her own child. "Aye, I'm at me wit's end to get the poor lass to cease workin' and enjoy life just a wee bit."

"Why, that *is* a problem, though a very strange one indeed," said the prince. "What sort of work does your daughter do?"

"Oh, every sort of chore that a fine woman would do, though the work that she does best is spinning, weaving, and sewing," answered the widow.

At this information the prince brightened, for he had been searching for a bride for nearly a year, and none he presented had suited his mother, the queen. His messen-gers had searched the length and breadth of Ireland for a maiden who could perform all the duties of a lady, especially spinning, weaving, and sewing. The queen was deter-mined that only the finest would be good enough for *her* son, but, alas, no maiden could be found to live up to her expectations.

"The problem here lies not with your daughter, but with you, old woman," charged the prince indignantly, "for not realizing what a jewel Eileen is. Why, my mes-sengers have searched all of Ireland for just such a maiden, and here she is, right under your nose!"

With that, the prince invited Eileen to ride with him to the palace to become his bride. Both the old widow and Eileen were astonished at the strange turn of events, but said nothing as the beaming Eileen got on the horse behind the prince and rode off with him to the palace.

The prince rushed into the palace with Eileen following along behind to introduce her to the queen.

"Mother, at long last I have the maiden we have been searching for. Eileen can spin and weave and sew and, what's more, is such a hard worker that her mother can barely get her to rest!" explained the prince in a rush of breath.

The queen, though unimpressed with her son's discovery, nodded courteously to Eileen.

"Welcome to the palace, young lady," said the queen. "My son's comments may very well prove true, but we will need to have you take the test, nevertheless."

The queen regally strode from the room with Eileen trailing her silently. She showed her to a room that contained a spinning wheel and a huge stack of raw silk.

"Spin all this silk into thread before nightfall," said the queen, who then left the room and locked the door.

Eileen sat down at the spinning wheel and began to weep, as she had never spun so much as an inch of thread in her entire life.

Before long, an old hag appeared in the room. She was ancient, and one of her feet was as big as a pillow. She watched Eileen sobbing for a bit and then inquired, "Young miss, why are you crying?"

Eileen stopped her weeping long enough to answer, "Because I must spin all this silk into thread by nightfall, or I will not be allowed to wed the prince."

"'Twill not be a problem," replied the hag, "I can spin the silk for you if you promise me one thing."

"Anything you ask," replied Eileen eagerly.

"Invite me to your wedding," said the hag.

Eileen quickly agreed and the old hag set to work, skillfully and rapidly spinning the silk into thread with her huge foot pressing the pedal of the spinning wheel.

Nightfall arrived and the queen returned to the room, quietly turning the key in the lock and entering.

"I see you were able to complete the task," said the queen coolly. "Let's see how well you perform tomorrow's chore."

The next day the queen had a loom brought into the room.

"Weave all this thread into cloth before nightfall," said the queen who then left the room and locked the door.

Eileen sat down, surveyed the pile of thread and the empty loom, and burst into tears, because she had never woven so much as a square inch of cloth before.

Before long a different old hag appeared in the room. Like the previous hag, she was ancient, though she had two normal-sized feet. However, she had one hand as big as a kettle. She watched Eileen sobbing for a bit and then inquired, "Young miss, why are you crying?"

Eileen stopped her weeping long enough to answer, "Because I must weave all this thread into cloth by nightfall, or I will not be allowed to wed the prince."

"'Twill not be a problem," replied the hag. "I can weave the cloth for you if you promise me one thing."

"Anything you ask," replied Eileen eagerly.

"Invite me to your wedding," said the hag.

Eileen quickly agreed, and the old hag set to work, skillfully throwing the shuttle and weaving the thread into cloth with her huge hand.

Nightfall arrived and the queen returned to the room, quietly turning the key in the lock and entering.

"I see you were able to complete the task," said the queen coolly. "Let's see how well you perform on tomorrow's chore."

The next day the queen had a needle, thimble, and scissors brought into the room.

"Sew all this cloth into shirts for the prince before nightfall," said the queen, who then left the room and locked the door.

Eileen sat down, surveyed the pile of cloth and the sewing equipment, and burst into tears, because she had never even threaded a needle before, much less, sewn a garment.

Before long, still a different old hag appeared in the room. Like the previous hags, she was ancient, though she had two normal-sized feet and two normal-sized hands. However, she had a nose as big as a goose's fanny. She watched Eileen sobbing for a bit and then inquired, "Why are you crying?"

Eileen stopped her weeping long enough to answer, "Because I must sew all this cloth into shirts by nightfall, or I will not be allowed to wed the prince."

"'Twill not be a problem," replied the hag. "I can sew the cloth into shirts for you if you promise me one thing."

"Anything you ask," replied Eileen eagerly.

"Invite me to your wedding," said the hag.

Eileen quickly agreed, and the old hag set to work, smoothly cutting and stitching the cloth into shirts with her heavy-nosed head bent over the work.

Nightfall arrived and the queen returned to the room, quietly turning the key in the lock and entering.

"I see you were able to complete this task also," said the astounded queen. "Very well, then. I can see that you will be a suitable bride for my son. He need never employ a spinner, a weaver, nor a seamstress while you are his wife."

So Eileen and the prince were wed. There were many guests at the lavish wedding feast and all were eating and drinking, except the one who should have been the happiest of all, Eileen. She could not enjoy her good fortune for thinking about what she would do if the prince asked her to spin or weave or sew.

Suddenly, a loud knock was heard on the door of the banquet hall. A servant opened the door, and the room fell silent as an ancient hag with one foot as big as a pillow hobbled in and made her way to the head table with the prince and the bride.

The prince, who had excellent manners, immediately stood and asked politely, "Good day, madam. Are you a guest of the groom or of the bride?"

"I'm a guest of the bride, sire," answered the old hag.

"Then welcome to our wedding. Please be so kind as to share in our banquet," said the prince courteously.

A servant quickly came up and escorted the old hag over to the tables of the bride's guests.

Finally curiosity overcame the prince, and he strolled over to where the old hag was enjoying her refreshments.

"If you don't mind my asking, madam," he began very politely. "I would like to know how your one foot came to be so much larger than the other."

"No, sire," answered the hag. "I do not mind your asking. In my younger days I ran a spinning wheel so much that all the blood rushed to this foot and made it the sight it is today."

At that the prince's eyes grew wide with astonishment.

"Then I will make a decree at this very moment," announced the prince firmly. "Never shall my bride so much as set foot to a spinning wheel so that this will never happen to her!"

The prince returned to his table with Eileen and resumed celebrating, certain that he had saved his bride from disaster.

Suddenly, a loud knock was heard on the door of the banquet hall. A servant opened the door, and the room fell silent as an ancient hag with one hand as big as a kettle hobbled in and made her way to the head table with the prince and the bride.

The prince, who had excellent manners, immediately stood and asked politely, "Good day, madam. Are you a guest of the groom or of the bride?"

"I'm a guest of the bride, sire," answered the old hag.

"Then welcome to our wedding. Please be so kind as to share in our banquet," said the prince courteously.

A servant quickly came up and escorted the old hag over to the tables of the bride's guests.

Finally curiosity overcame the prince, and he strolled over to where the old hag was enjoying her refreshments.

"If you don't mind my asking, madam," he began very politely. "I would like to know how your one hand came to be so much larger than the other."

"No, sire," answered the hag, "I do not mind your asking. In my younger days I wove at a loom so much that all the blood rushed to this hand and made it the sight it is today."

At that the prince's eyes grew wide with astonishment.

"Then I will make a decree at this very moment," announced the prince firmly. "Never shall my bride so much as set hand to a loom so that this will never happen to her!"

The prince returned to his table with Eileen and resumed celebrating, certain that he had saved his bride from disaster.

Suddenly, a loud knock was heard on the door of the banquet hall. A servant opened the door, and the room fell silent as yet another ancient hag with a nose as big as a goose's fanny shuffled in and made her way to the head table with the prince and the bride.

The prince, who had excellent manners, immediately stood and asked politely, "Good day, madam. Are you a guest of the groom or of the bride?"

"I'm a guest of the bride, sire," answered the old hag.

"Then welcome to our wedding. Please be so kind as to share in our banquet," said the prince courteously.

A servant quickly came up and escorted the old hag over to the tables of the bride's guests.

Finally curiosity overcame the prince, and he strolled over to where the old hag was enjoying her refreshments.

"If you don't mind my asking, madam," he began very politely. "I would like to know how your nose came to be so large."

"No, sire," answered the hag, "I do not mind your asking. In my younger days I kept my head bent over so much sewing that all the blood rushed to my nose and made it the sight it is today."

At that the prince's eyes grew wide with astonishment.

"Then I will make a decree at this very moment," announced the prince firmly. "Never shall my bride so much as thread a needle or do any other kind of household work, so that this will never happen to her!"

The prince returned to his table with Eileen and resumed celebrating, certain that he had saved his bride from disaster.

Eileen's heart rejoiced, for now she would be able to spend her life doing what she did best—nothing. The prince was always watching to make certain that Eileen did not endanger herself by doing any household work. But she never did, thus saving herself from certain disaster.

# Discussion Questions

### Prereading Questions

Unlike the folktales in most of the other units, these four stories probably all evolved from the original German "Rumpelstiltskin." The story may have been retold first in England, where it was changed only slightly—mainly the name of the little creature. When the tale was retold in Cornwall and Ireland, however, it became a parody of the original. What is a parody?

### Reading Focus Question

As you listen to the two folktales "Rumpelstiltskin" and "Tom Tit Tot," think about what they teach the listener about honesty. The other two tales, "Eileen and the Three Hags" and "Duffy and the Devil," seem to to teach either a different lesson or perhaps no lesson at all. What do you think about these two stories?

### Post-Reading Questions

(Return to Focus Question) What was the lesson learned in "Rumpelstiltskin" and "Tom Tit Tot"? What was the lesson learned in "Eileen and the Three Hags" and "Duffy and the Devil"? Did you chuckle when you heard those tales? What do you think was the purpose of telling those two folktales?

# Spinning Tales Map

*Directions:* Find the continent for each folktale. Choose a colored pencil or fine-tipped marker to color both the continent and the matching box in the legend.

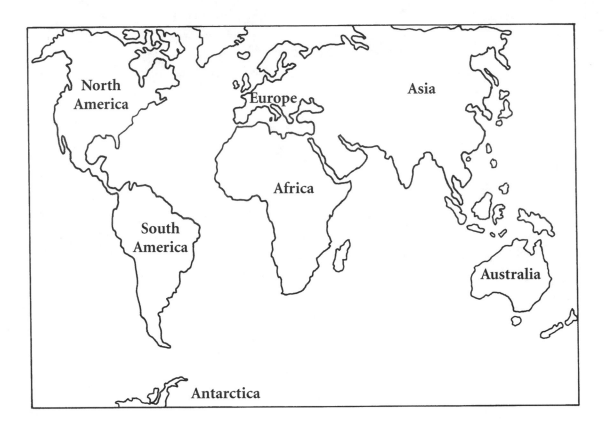

☐ Germany ("Rumpelstiltskin")

☐ Ireland ("Eileen and the Three Hags")

☐ England ("Tom Tit Tot")

☐ Cornwall ("Duffy and the Devil")

Copyright © 1999 Linda K. Garrity • *The Tale Spinner*
Fulcrum Publishing • (800) 992-2908 • www.fulcrum-resources.com

_____

# Spinning Wheel

*Directions:* Color the spinning wheel and the girl. Then cut out the wheel and attach it at the center with a brad. Draw your idea of Rumpelstiltskin, Tom Tit Tot, the devil, or the three hags in the empty space next to the girl. Write the name of the imaginary creature beneath your drawing. Then cut around the dotted lines to complete your picture. How different is each person's idea of the imaginary character?

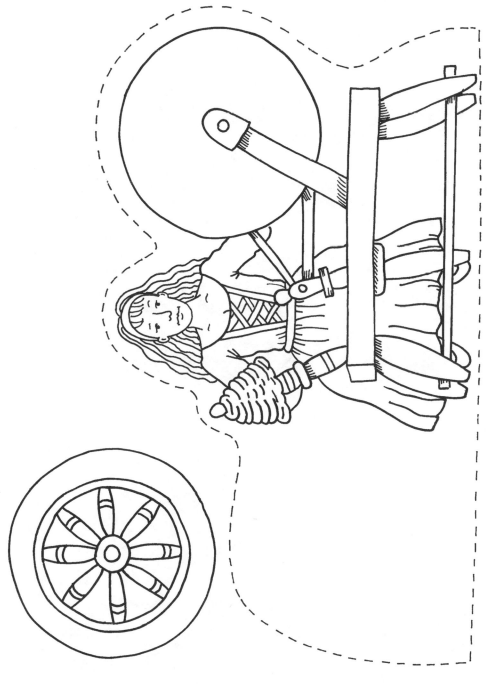

# Special "Three" Ball

*Directions:* Folklore from all cultures uses the number "three." There are often three characters, three wishes, three challenges, or events happening three times. Choose an example of "threeness" from one of the stories that you've heard and illustrate it on three of the triangles. Write the title of the tale on the fourth triangle. Cut out the circles, fold them at the dashed lines, and glue flaps together to form a ball.

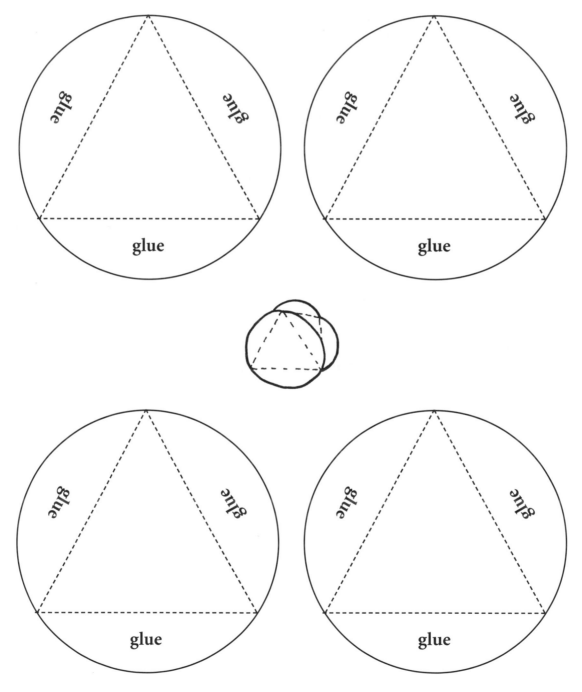

# Make-Believe Research

*Directions:* In the "Spinning Tales" variants, the little imaginary character has different names and appearances. Different cultures have unique magical characters. Research a magical character. Describe it, tell which culture started it, and in what folktales it is featured. Then draw a picture of it. Here are some ideas: genies, gnomes, leprechauns, trolls, dragons, banshees, giants, elves, uldas, gremlins, hobgoblins, pixies, changelings, nisses, brownies, barbegazis, and fairies.

## Spinning Tales Photo Album

*Directions:* Create a photo album for one of the folktales. Color the cover to look like leather, cut it out and glue it to heavy paper. Trace the cover onto heavy paper to make a back. Start with pictures of the earliest events of the story and end with the final event. Bind the album together with string or yarn.

→
continued

## Spinning Tales Photo Album (continued)

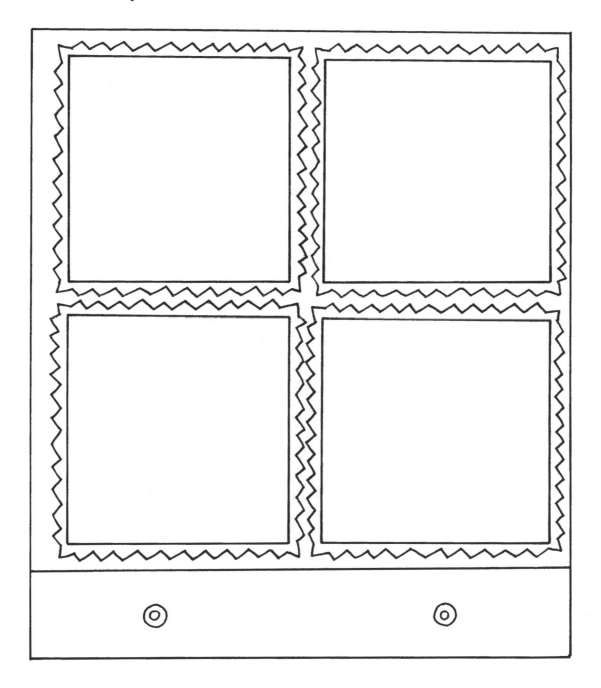

# Bibliography

Crossley-Holland, Kevin. *British Folk Tales*. New York: Franklin Watts, 1987.

> This book has an excellent version of the British variant "Tom Tit Tot."

Galdone, Paul. *Rumpelstiltskin*. New York: Clarion Books, 1985.

> Galdone's version, which is very close to the original, is an excellent choice for group use because of the large size of the book and illustrations. The bright colors and large, expressive faces make this tale come alive for even those in the back row.

Grimm, Jacob. *Rumpelstiltskin*. New York: Holiday House, 1983.

> Donna Diamond's incredible pencil drawings look almost like photographs. Her vision of Rumpelstiltskin shows him as a small man, not an imaginary character. The retelling is close to the original and the illustrations strike quite a contrast to other versions.

Grimm, Jacob. *Rumpelstiltskin*. Englewood Cliffs, N.J.: Prentice-Hall, 1984.

> John Wallner takes a very different approach to illustration than Donna Diamond's realism. In his images, the fantasy aspect of the tale emphasized by adding bats, dragons, and assorted gargoyles to the medieval-influenced pictures. The rich color and framed paintings make this an attractive version.

Langley, Jonathan. *Rumpelstiltskin*. New York: HarperCollins, 1991.

> This whimsical edition by the British author Jonathan Langley retains the original storyline though it borders closely on parody, especially in the updated ending where the greedy king gets his final and justly deserved "reward." The droll illustrations perfectly match the witty and lively style of the book.

Ness, Evaline. *Tom Tit Tot: An English Folk Tale*. New York: Scribner's, 1965.

> Lively woodcut illustrations by Evaline Ness bring Joseph Jacob's folktale from *English Folk and Fairy Tales* to life. The many words and phrases from the vernacular add to the flavor of the tale. The main difference between this story and "Rumpelstiltskin" is that the object of the creature's desire in "Tom Tit Tot" is the maiden herself, not her firstborn child.

Sage, Alison. *Rumpelstiltskin.* New York: Dial Books, 1991.

> The exquisite paintings done in the style of European medieval tapestries by the Russian artist Gennady Spirin make this edition unique. Sage's retelling expands slightly upon the original text in various places and, along with the detailed illustrations, captivates the audience.

Tarcov, Edith H. *Rumpelstiltskin.* New York: Scholastic, 1973.

> Tarcov's faithful retelling combined with Gorey's droll illustrations have long kept this paperback version in print.

Zelinsky, Paul O. *Rumpelstiltskin.* New York: Dutton, 1986.

> The paintings in Zelinsky's picture book are so captivating and realistic that one can empathize with the miller's daughter's anguish and elation, almost touch the patina of the wooden spinning wheel, and feel amazement at the burnished spindles of spun gold. Zelinsky used three different manuscripts from early collections by the Grimm Brothers as a basis for the text. Care and pride are readily apparent in this Caldecott Honor book.

Zemach, Harve. *Duffy and the Devil.* New York: Farrar, Straus, Giroux, 1973.

> The Zemachs (Margot as illustrator) have teamed up to present a humorous, rollicking variant from Cornwall. The humor and energetic illustrations will appeal greatly to children, who closely follow this story right to the hilarious final page. This story is available in audiocassette as well.

### Parodies

Moser, Barry. *Tucker Pfeffercorn.* Boston: Little, Brown, 1994.

> Set in the rural South, Moser's realistic, haunting paintings perfectly complement this highly creative modern parody.

Scieszka, Jonn, and Lane Smith. *The Stinky Cheese Man and Other Fairly Stupid Tales.* New York: Viking Penguin, 1992.

> If you are looking for a bizarre parody for all the tales in this book except "The Brementown Musicians," this is it! Winner of a 1992 Caldecott Honor book award, *The Stinky Cheese Man ...* is quite unique and not uniformly admired by adults, though it tickles childrens' funnybones.

Stanley, Diane. *Rumpelstiltskin's Daughter*. New York: Morrow, 1997.

In this large, ornately illustrated picture book the original story is parodied and then carried further with the next generation. Rather than become victims of the greedy king, the spunky miller's daughter and later her bright, good-hearted daughter dupe the foolish king and end up being able to help the peasants. A clever book that will generate quality discussion about the roles of females in fairytales!

Velde, Vivian Vande. *Tales from the Brothers Grimm and the Sisters Weird*. San Diego: Harcourt, 1995.

The bizarre cover on this story collection does a disservice to the sensitive folk-tale parodies inside. "Straw into Gold" is an outstanding parody of "Rumpelstiltskin" that will receive avid attention and generate spirited discussion.

# Chapter 7

# Cooperation Pays

## Introduction

Several cultures have animal folktales with the theme of the animals working together to escape death and to create a new life for themselves. Some of the tales portray the animals as musicians, and all of them have a conclusion with the animals working together to fool and drive out an intruder of some kind. This set of folktales is probably the most similar of any set in the book, leading one to believe that they are all variants of one original tale. Which story was the original is impossible to tell, but they are all entertaining to hear.

### *Geography*

Use the "Cooperation Pays Map" activity to familiarize the children with the locations of the source countries for this unit's folktales.

### *Art*

"Animal Collage" is a creative art activity that involves tearing colored paper to create an interesting tree. The project can be done entirely with child-created animals or the reproducible ones which are from "The Brementown Musicians" (see Bibliography for listing of versions, pages 120–121). Or boys and girls could choose their favorite folktale from the unit to use as the basis for their collage. They should label the project with the title of the tale and the culture.

"Animal Pop-Up" is a simple craft activity designed for younger children, who are thrilled at the chance to make pop-ups. Though the sample shows animals from "The Brementown Musicians," any tale from the unit can be used.

### Writing

"Letters to the Editor" is designed as a higher-level thinking and writing activity. Bring in examples from real newspapers to share with the children in preparation for this activity. It can be difficult for one individual to think of both sides of an argument. It might be easier for two children to work together on this project with each one taking an opposing view. Three examples of controversial topics related to the folktales are given on the activity page, but more topics can be brainstormed.

### Comprehension

"Story Wheel" will be too challenging for younger children. This requires a high level of comprehension and sequencing skills, in addition to well-developed fine motor skills. A good activity for cooperative-learning groups, the tasks for this project can be divided in each group with some children doing the artwork and some doing the text.

### Critical Thinking

Compare the beginning sentences of each of these folktales. Which beginning tells you immediately that this a folk or fairy tale? Cultures have unique beginnings and endings to their folktales. One ending that is delightful is the one used in many Scandinavian tales. If you look up a copy of "The Three Billy Goats Gruff," you will find that the last sentence reads, "Snip, snap, snout, this tale's told out." Children could research folktale books in the media center to discover different beginnings and endings.

### Puppetry

The folktales in this unit lend themselves to puppet plays due to the large number of animals and dialogue in all the tales. Simple paper-bag puppets would work for any age. A drama activity like this is great fun and also builds important skills such as memorization, sequencing, and speech.

# The Brementown Musicians (Germany)

nce upon a time there lived a donkey who was so old and tired that he could no longer haul sacks of grain to the mill for his owner.

One day he overheard his master say, "There is no point in feeding a useless animal. I will sell this beast to the butcher tomorrow."

That night the donkey decided that he should run away before his owner sold him. But where should he go? What could he do to earn a living?

"I have always loved music, and given a chance, I know I could play the lute," considered the donkey. "I know, I'll go to Brementown and join the band!"

So bright and early the next morning the donkey set forth on his new life. As he ambled along, he noticed a brown lump up ahead on the road. When the donkey finally reached the lump, he was startled to realize that it was an old hound.

"What are you doing out here?" questioned the alarmed donkey.

"I am too old and slow to run the hunt with my master," answered the dog sorrowfully. "So I ran off before he could kill me. But now I don't know what to do to make a living."

"I know," answered the donkey brightly. "You could go with me to Brementown. I was in the same situation with my master until I decided to run away and join the band as a lute player."

"That's a wonderful idea," said the dog. "Let's see. I've always wanted to play the drums."

"And a fine drummer you would be," exclaimed the donkey, as the two headed merrily on down the road to Brementown.

As the two ambled along, they noticed a small gray lump up ahead on the road. When the animals finally reached the lump, they were startled to realize that it was an old house cat.

"What are you doing out here?" questioned the donkey and the dog.

"I am too old and toothless to catch mice for my mistress," answered the cat sorrowfully, "so I ran off before she could kill me. But now I don't know what to do to make a living."

"I know," answered the donkey brightly. "You could go with us to Brementown. I was in the same situation with my master until I decided to run away and join the band as a lute player. The hound here is going to play the drums. What instrument can you play?"

"That's a wonderful idea," said the cat. "Let's see. I don't have much talent for instruments like you two animals, but people have often commented on my high-pitched voice. I think I could sing soprano with the band."

"And a fine singer you would be," exclaimed the donkey and the hound, as the three headed merrily on down the road to Brementown.

As the three ambled along, they noticed a small brown and white lump up ahead on the road. When the animals finally reached the lump, they were startled to realize that it was an old rooster.

"What are you doing out here?" questioned the donkey, the dog and the cat.

"I am old and my master wants to make soup out of me," answered the rooster sorrowfully. "So I ran off before he could kill me. But now I don't know what to do to make a living."

"I know," answered the donkey brightly. "You could go with us to Brementown. We were all in similar situations with our masters until we decided to run away and join the Brementown band. I am going to become a lute player. The hound here is going to play the drums and the cat will, naturally, sing soprano. What instrument can you play?"

"That's a wonderful idea," said the rooster. "Let's see. I don't have much talent for instruments like you two animals, but people have often commented on my loud voice. I think I could sing bass with the band."

"And a fine singer you would be," exclaimed the other animals, as they headed merrily on down the road to Brementown.

The foursome was not speedy enough to reach Brementown in one day, and so by nightfall, all were too tired to continue. At first the animals settled down for the night in and around a large tree. The dog and donkey laid down under the tree, and the cat and rooster chose branches for themselves. But just then the rooster, being perched on a high branch, spied a snug cabin with inviting smoke curling out of the chimney.

" Friends, there is a warm cabin up ahead. Let's see if we can spend the night and perhaps have a bite to eat there."

They all agreed that this was a wonderful idea and trotted right up to a large window on the side of the cabin. The donkey propped his hooves on the windowsill to look inside the home.

"What do you see?" asked the cat impatiently, as she was accustomed to sitting next to a cozy fire in the evenings.

"Well, I do see a fine table spread with plenty to eat and drink," answered the donkey, "but I also see a band of evil robbers eating it all."

The hound, who was good at plans, thought for a minute, and then explained his clever plan to rid the cabin of knaves. The donkey stood firmly with his hooves on the windowsill. Then the dog climbed onto his back and the cat, mindful of her claws, gently climbed upon the back of the dog. Finally, the rooster flew up and perched on the top of the cat. At the dog's signal, all four animals made music together. And what music it was! The donkey brayed, the dog barked, the cat meowed, and the rooster crowed as loudly as they could.

The robbers, hearing such an unearthly sound, jumped out of their chairs and fled into the forest, fearing for their very lives. So then the four musicians, seeing that the coast was clear, sauntered on into the cabin to enjoy an elegant, relaxing dinner. After the fine meal, they were all ready for a good night's sleep. The rooster flew up to a rafter beam for a comfortable perch. The cat curled up on the hearth. The dog stretched out on the doormat, and the donkey laid down in the grassy front yard.

Meanwhile, the robbers, becoming cold and uncomfortable, decided to investigate what had become of their cozy cabin. The leader sent one of his men back in the dark of night to check out the cabin.

With the cabin being so dark the robber decided to light a candle by touching it to one of the hot coals in the fireplace. Mistaking the glowing eyes of the cat for coals, the robber stuck the candle in one of them. At that the cat leaped into the air, clawing and hissing.

The terrified robber, trying to get away from the cat, tripped over the dog, who jumped up and bit the man's leg. The robber lumbered out the front door of the cabin only to be met by the sharp hooves of the donkey.

Just as the robber sped away from the place, he heard the rooster crow, "Cock a doodle doo! Cock a doodle doo!"

When the robber reached his fellow thieves hiding in the forest, he told them all about the harrowing time he suffered in the cabin, "I tell you, that place is haunted. First a wicked witch scratched me with her long claws. Then a ghost stabbed me in the leg with a knife. As I ran through the yard, some kind of black monster hit me with a big club. There was a judge sitting in the rafters who screamed, "Kill the rogue, do!"

With that the robbers fled from the area, never to return.

And as for the four animals, they all enjoyed living in the cabin and making fine music together so much that they stayed and lived happily ever after.

# Jack and the Traveling Animals (Ireland)

he day came when Jack and his poor widowed mother had very little to eat. Young Jack decided it was time to seek his fortune so he could help his poor old mother. Though she was sad to see him go, his mother baked him some bread and gave him her blessing.

Jack traveled through the morning until he came upon a man beating his donkey. Jack quickly grabbed the club from the man and whacked him with it until he fled.

The donkey was indeed grateful, "Thank ye, kind sir. That rogue was not my master. He stole me away and has been beating me ever since."

"It's glad I am to be able to help you," said the good-hearted Jack.

"And where would you be off to this mornin'?" inquired the donkey.

"I'm off to seek my fortune in the world," replied Jack.

"Would you like the company of an old donkey?" asked the donkey politely.

"Aye, that I would," answered Jack and the two set off down the road.

They hadn't traveled very far when, from over the hill, came such clanking and yelping as to raise the dead. As Jack and the donkey ambled a little closer, they saw a bedraggled little dog with a collection of cans tied to his tail. Jack quickly bent down, held the dog tightly, and untied the cans. Then he put the frightened animal back down.

"Thank ye kindly, sir," spoke the dog. "Some ruffians in the next village tormented me to provide merriment for themselves."

"It's glad I am to be able to help you," said the good-hearted Jack.

"And where would you be off to this mornin'?" inquired the dog.

"I'm off to seek my fortune in the world," replied Jack.

"Would you like the company of a little dog?" asked the dog politely.

"Aye, that I would," answered Jack, and the three set off down the road.

The trio hadn't traveled very far when they came upon a cat with its paw caught in a rabbit trap, crying piteously. Quick as a wink, Jack was bent over the pathetic animal, releasing its paw and comforting it. He tore off the bottom of his own shirt to make bandages and then cleaned and wrapped the cat's paw. At last Jack put the scrawny cat back down.

"Thank ye kindly, sir," said the cat gratefully.

"It's glad I am to be able to help you," said the good-hearted Jack.

"And where would you be off to this mornin'?" inquired the cat.

"I'm off to seek my fortune in the world," replied Jack.

"Would you like the company of a scrawny cat?" asked the cat politely.

"Aye, that I would," answered Jack, and the four set off down the road.

They hadn't traveled very far before they came across a rooster, crowing and carrying on as if Judgment Day was upon him.

"What is the matter, my feathered friend?" asked Jack anxiously.

"I'm lost, I tell ye. I set off early this morning to see the world and now I don't know where I am," said the dismayed rooster.

"You're right where you are," explained Jack.

"Really?" said the rooster. "I wouldn't know, for I've not been to school."

"Indeed," answered Jack. "You're right here on this fencepost."

"Thank ye kindly, sir," said the rooster gratefully.

"It's glad I am to be able to help you," said the good-hearted Jack.

"And where would you be off to this mornin'?" inquired the rooster.

"I'm off to seek my fortune in the world," replied Jack.

"Would you like the company of a silly rooster?" asked the rooster politely.

"Aye, that I would," answered Jack, and the five set off down the road.

The group traveled together for the rest of the day until night began to settle upon the countryside. A wee cottage near the road looked like an inviting place to spend the night. As the group approached the cottage, they encountered a man sitting on a stool outside the house, looking forlorn as a stormy night.

"God bless you, sir," said Jack politely.

"And God bless you and your fine company," returned the man. "Where might you be off to this evenin'?"

"We're off to seek our fortunes in the world and were wondering if we might spend the night in your wee snug cottage?" asked Jack.

"If the cottage were just mine to loan," sighed the man.

"You mean the cottage behind you is not your own?" asked Jack.

"Well, it is and it isn't," answered the man. "You see, I hold title to the cottage, but just today my wife's relatives have descended upon us for the entire summer. So I'm sittin' out here with me own black thoughts."

"It's sorry I am for you, sir," said the good-hearted Jack, as he and the animals started on down the road.

"Wait!" called out the man. "There's no reason you and your comrades can't sleep in the kitchen tonight. Everyone is fast asleep. Just be certain to be gone before daybreak when the grumpy old grandmother awakes."

Jack gratefully assured the man that they would be long gone by the first streak of light. He and the animals settled about the kitchen and quickly fell sound asleep.

All went well until the middle of the night when the grandmother awoke and came out to the dark kitchen for a bite of something to eat. Upon entering the darkened room, she stepped on the dog, who howled and bit her leg. The old biddy screamed and leaped into the air, coming down upon the cat, who screeched, flew up and clawed her arm. All of this commotion frightened the rooster, who flew over to the old lady's head and landed on it, digging in with its sharp claws. Finally, the donkey reared back and kicked her in the seat of the pants with both hind hooves, sending the cantankerous old woman right out the door. By this time the rest of the household was awake and trying to discover what was happening.

"Don't stay one minute longer in this lunatic asylum!" screamed the old woman. "Pack your bags, all of you, in a flash, and let's be gone from here and never darken these doors again."

The old grandmother and her relatives were quickly packed and down the road. Jack and his companions were the heroes of the night, for the couple was overjoyed to be rid of their obnoxious relatives. Jars of ale and whisky were brought forth, and food for both people and beasts was served. The group sang and feasted the rest of the night.

The next morning the man offered Jack and the animals jobs on the farm. The all worked hard, and Jack was able to provide for his poor widowed mother.

Eventually, the farmer's beautiful daughter fell in love with Jack, for he was as handsome as he was good hearted. They were married, and the four animals stood up with Jack and were greatly admired by all. They were all very happy and never knew one day less happy during all of their lives thereafter.

# The Traveling Musicians (Puerto Rico)

nce there was a peasant with an old burro who was so old that he could no longer pull a cart. The burro overheard the peasant tell his wife that he was going to kill the decrepit animal, so the old burro ran away that very night.

As he was ambling along, far from home, he encountered a goat, chewing on his rope.

"Qué pasa (What's happening), cabra vieja (*cob* bruh vee *ay* haw) (old goat)?" asked the burro.

"I am trying to free myself," answered the goat as he chewed frantically. "My master is going to kill me tomorrow, as I have grown old and useless."

"Here, let me help you with that rope, cabra vieja," said the burro, and together they soon had the rope severed and were trotting on down the road. The two animals hadn't traveled too far before they encountered an exhausted, panting dog.

"Qué pasa, perro viejo (old dog)?" asked the burro.

"I have been running away from home," answered the dog. "My master is going to kill me since I have grown old and useless."

"Then come along with us, perro viejo," offered the burro.

The animals exchanged their stories and soon were all trotting down the road amiably.

Before long they encountered a cat, meowing woefully.

"Qué pasa, gato (*gaw* toe) viejo (old cat)?" asked the burro.

"I have run away from home because I am no longer able to catch mice, and I feared my owner would kill me," explained the cat. "Now I am weak from hunger."

"Then come along with us," offered the burro. "For we have had similar situations."

At that the cat joined the merry little band as they began to search for a safe shelter for the night. They soon found a large tree and began to settle within and beneath it. As they started to nod off, they were abruptly awakened by the crowing of a rooster in a high limb.

"Whoa, el gallo (*gaw* yo) (rooster), mi amigo (my friend). Why are you crowing at this time of the night, rather than the morning?" asked the burro.

"Since I am so old, my master is going to kill me tomorrow morning for soup, so I thought I would get in my last crowing tonight," answered the rooster.

"You should join us animals, el gallo viejo," said the burro. "We are all fleeing ungrateful men after long years of loyal service. Starting tomorrow morning, we are going to travel and enjoy ourselves."

The band of animals was true to this pledge. But after a few days, the animals tired of the life of leisure and began to discuss what they could do to be useful. After a lifetime of service, it would not be easy to be idle. After discussing their talents, they decided that they would be ideally suited as musicians. The burro wanted to play a guitar and the goat wanted to play the drums with his little hooves. The cat, naturally, would sing soprano and the dog would sing bass. The rooster, with his marvelous voice, would be the lead singer.

After much practicing, the traveling musicians were finally ready to present their first serenade. The rooster flew ahead to the first house with a light in the window. As the window was quite high, the animals had to stand upon one another's backs to reach the window sill. Finally, they were ready to perform. At a signal from the rooster they all burst into lively song, complete with extra verses.

Unbeknown to the musicians, a group of robbers was inside the house counting their loot. Upon hearing the lively concert, these rogues fled the house thinking that soldiers had come to capture them.

The musicians, seeing their audience fleeing the concert, were distressed. So, to comfort themselves, they went on in the house and ate the food left by the robbers. At last they all found a comfortable spot, put out the lights, and went to sleep.

The robbers decided to send one of their band back to the house to see if the soldiers were gone. The house appeared dark and quiet, so the robber walked right on in. In fact, the house appeared so dark that the robber decided to light a match on a live coal. He reached his match for one of the two bright glowing spots near the fireplace. ¡Aiyeh! It was the glowing eyes of the cat with claws like a sharp dagger who cut the robber's hand. As he moved back from that danger, the burro kicked him into the next room, then the goat butted him to the door, where the dog bit his leg, and finally, the rooster flew at his head, clawing him with his talons.

By the time the robber got back to his companions, he was bleeding and very frightened. He told them that there were rogues inside who stabbed him, kicked him, struck him with a sword, and attacked him with a hatchet. The robbers needed no more convincing about the viciousness of the rogues and abandoned the area immediately.

The animals continued to live in the house in great comfort, making beautiful music each evening. No neighbors disturbed the musicians, thinking that the nightly serenade was the work of the devil.

# The Ox and His Animal Friends (Russia)

The peasant and his wife were expecting relatives for the Easter celebration. Early the day before, the peasant and his wife discussed the various dishes that she was going to prepare for their guests the following day.

"Our rooster has become old, but would be delicious to serve at the holy feast," said the wife.

"Very well," said her husband as he marched off to the barnyard to butcher the rooster.

The rooster, however, had overheard the conversation and fled to the forest.

The peasant returned to the hut and explained to his wife, "I searched in every nook and cranny, but could not find the rooster anywhere."

"That is most strange, but do not fret. Roast goose would be even more grand to serve to our guests. Go back out and butcher the goose," said the wife.

"Very well," said her husband as he marched off to the barnyard to butcher the goose.

The goose, however, had overheard the conversation and fled to the forest.

The peasant returned to the hut and explained to his wife, "I searched in every nook and cranny but could not find the goose anywhere."

"That is most strange, but do not fret. Roast mutton would be even more grand to serve to our guests. Go back and butcher the sheep," said the wife.

"Very well," said her husband as he marched off to the barnyard to butcher the sheep."

The sheep, however, had overheard the conversation and fled to the forest.

The peasant returned to the hut and explained to his wife, "I searched in every nook and cranny, but could not find the sheep anywhere."

"That is most strange, but do not fret. Roast pork would be even more grand to serve to our guests. Go back and butcher the pig," said the wife.

The pig, however, had overheard the conversation and fled to the forest.

The peasant returned to the hut and explained to his wife, "I searched in every nook and cranny, but could not find the pig anywhere."

"That is most strange strange, but do not fret, there is still the ox," said the wife.

The peasant was most reluctant to butcher his largest and only remaining animal, but slowly walked back to the barnyard.

But the ox, too, had overheard the conversation and fled to the forest to join the other animals.

The five animals enjoyed their carefree life in the forest that spring and summer. Food was plentiful and none had to worry about being served up as a holiday meal.

As autumn began to rustle through the forest, the ox became concerned, as winter in the forests of Russia is very severe.

"Comrades, winter will soon be at our heels. We must work to build ourselves a hut and set aside food," warned the large animal.

"I have no need of a hut," answered the sheep. "This thick woolen coat will protect me from all weather."

"Winter weather does not bother me," the pig assured the ox. "I will simple use my snout and tusks to dig a cozy burrow in the earth and stay there."

"No problem for me either," added the goose. "I merely tuck my head under a wing and those winter winds blow right on by."

"I'll just find shelter in the heavy branches of the evergreens, so winter is not a problem," said the rooster nonchalantly.

"Then I shall have to build the hut myself," said the ox as he started to work.

The ox eventually completed the hut, and a fine Russian wooden hut it was. Snug and tight, it even had a warm stone stove and plenty of wood.

As so often happens, the leisurely warmth of autumn turned savage with heavy snow and icy blasts.

It wasn't long before the long, bitterly cold nights were taking their toll on the other four animals.

"Baaaa!" cried the sheep outside the door of the ox's warm hut. "Let me in!"

But, dear sheep, where is your thick woolen coat that protects you from all weather?" asked the ox innocently.

"Let me in or I will break down your door!" roared the foul-tempered sheep, remembering all too well his previous boasting.

"Very well, then," conceded the ox, who opened the door. The sheep rushed in to stand before the warm stove.

"Oink!" squealed the pig outside the door of the ox's warm hut. "Let me in!"

"But, dear pig, where is your snug burrow that protects you from all weather?" asked the ox innocently.

"Let me in or I will break down your door!" roared the foul-tempered pig, remembering all too well his previous boasting.

"Very well, then," conceded the ox, who opened the door The pig rushed in to stand before the warm stove.

"Squonk!" honked the goose outside the door of the ox's warm hut. "Let me in!"

"But, dear goose, where are your warm feathered wings that protect you as the winter winds blow by?" asked the ox innocently.

"Let me in or I will peck out the moss in the cracks!" roared the foul-tempered goose, remembering all too well her previous boasting.

"Very well, then," conceded the ox, who opened the door. The goose flew in and settled on a shelf near the warm stove.

"Cock a doodle do!" crowed the rooster outside the door of the ox's warm hut. "Let me in!"

"But, dear rooster, where are those winter branches that protect you from winter weather?" asked the ox innocently.

"Let me in or I will peck holes in your roof!" roared the foul-tempered rooster, remembering all too well his previous boasting.

"Very well, then," conceded the ox, who opened the door. The rooster flew in and settled on a wall peg near the warm stove.

The five animals lived together fairly peacefully as the cold winds howled outside the hut. But their peace and happiness was not to last throughout the winter, for a wolf and a bear heard about the group living together in the snug hut.

"Let us hurry to this hut in the forest, eat the tasty inhabitants, and then live there in comfort ourselves," suggested the wolf, whose mouth watered at the prospect of such a banquet.

"Delay no longer!" urged the hungry bear, so the animals sped to the ox's warm wooden hut.

Once there, however, their courage began to falter.

"You go on in first," said the wolf, "for you are so much larger."

"Oh, no, it should be you," argued the bear. "I am so clumsy, while you are agile and canny."

At last the wolf agreed to be the first in and forced open the door of the hut, while the bear waited back in the trees. The hut was completely dark, so the wolf stood there for a second, trying to get his bearings.

Bam! The ox and pig hurtled their sturdy bodies across the room, jamming the wolf against the wall.

Boom! The sheep lowered its head and butted the wolf up into the air.

Squock! Just as the wolf came down, the goose and rooster flew up and pecked him in the head, clawed his face, and swatted him with their wings.

The wolf, frightened as well as scratched and battered, twisted loose and dashed out of the hut into the forest. He finally caught up with the bear, who had run away after hearing all the clamor coming from the hut.

"Count yourself lucky that you did not go into that den of rogues!" exclaimed the bedraggled wolf to the bear. "Two huge peasants pinned me against a wall while a little one in a fur coat kicked me into the air. Then a tall one in a white babushka stabbed me with a knife while another tall one in a red and white babushka poked me with daggers and hit me with branches! I tell you, I barely escaped with my life!"

From that time on, the wolf and the bear stayed away from the hut in the forest and the five animals may be there still, or so I've been told.

# The Bull and His Animal Friends (Slovenia)

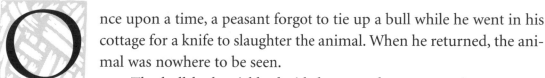nce upon a time, a peasant forgot to tie up a bull while he went in his cottage for a knife to slaughter the animal. When he returned, the animal was nowhere to be seen.

The bull had quickly decided to use the opportunity to escape and seek his fortune in the world. He had not gone far before he met a dog who had also run away.

"What are you doing on the roadway traveling all alone?" asked the dog.

"I'm going out into the world to seek my fortune," answered the bull rather importantly.

"May I go with you, as I too would like to seek my fortune?" asked the dog.

"Very well," answered the bull, "as long as you pull your own weight."

Before the pair had ambled down the road very far, they met a donkey who wanted to join them. And before long they were joined by a cat and, finally, a rooster. All were seeking their fortunes in the world, and all promised to pull their own weight.

When darkness came upon the band of travelers, they began to search for a good place to spend the night. This part of the roadway led through a deserted area of the forest where there were few farms. They finally spotted a light coming from a cottage. As they neared the cottage, they could hear the sounds of merriment coming from within. The bull, being the leader, peeked through the window and quickly realized that inside was a band of robbers counting their spoils and enjoying a feast.

The animals discussed what to do, and then decided that they should go to all the windows in the cottage and try to frighten the robbers by making their loudest sounds. The dog climbed up on the bull and the cat climbed up on the donkey, and they positioned themselves in front of two windows. The rooster perched on a low branch in front of a third window. At the bull's signal, they all belted out their loudest sounds. The bellowing, barking, braying, meowing, and crowing created an incredibly frightening noise. The robbers poured out of the cottage and fled into the forest.

The animals slowly entered the cottage and were astounded at the marvelous food and drink awaiting them, plus the piles of gold and jewels on the floor. They quickly came on in and held their own feast, each eating food to his own liking.

Meanwhile the robbers had stopped running through the forest and gathered together to make plans. They decided to send their leader back into the cottage to find out who or what had routed them from their den so quickly.

The animals, having eaten their fill at the feast, spread out around the cottage to sleep the rest of the night away. One of the robbers crept back into the dark cottage, unaware of the sleeping animals. The dog, sleeping by the door, jumped up and bit him ferociously in the leg. The robber saw two glowing embers just ahead and thought he would stir up the coals to create some light in the room. As he reached toward the coals, he poked the cat in the eyes and she flew up and scratched him furiously. As the robber turned around to flee, the bull came up and poked him with his two sharp horns. Spinning away from the horns, the hapless robber was met by two sharp hooves which kicked him right out the front door. Not wanting the other animals to think that he didn't pull his own weight, the rooster flew up and landed on the robber's head, clawing his face. At that, the robber screamed and fled to the forest.

The band of robbers was astonished at the sight of their bloody, frightened leader. "What ever was it in the cottage that attacked you so?" they asked anxiously.

"'Twas the very devil himself!" exclaimed the shaken man. "He first attacked my leg, trying to bite it off. Then he stabbed me with daggers, then with two sharp swords, and finally he threw me out with two pitchforks. Then he attacked my head with sharp nails. I'm not afraid of many men, but I'm no match for the devil!"

With that the robbers took flight through the forest and may be running still.

The five animals, realizing that they had found their fortunes, lived happily together in the cottage from that day forth with each one pulling his own weight.

# Discussion Questions

## *Prereading Questions*

- What does cooperation mean? The title of this theme is "Cooperation Pays." Give some examples where cooperation has paid off for you.

## *Reading Focus Question*

- As you listen to each of these animal folktales, think of how each folktale proves the expression "Cooperation Pays."

## *Post-Reading Questions*

- (Return to Focus Question) How did the characters cooperate with one another? Was it always easy? In which story did cooperation prove to be an especially big challenge?

- These folktales also used repetition and accumulation to build the stories. Give examples of both.

- Two folktales in this section have language that is unique to their culture. Which folktales? What words or phrases make the language unique?

- In each folktale one animal or person was the leader. What or who was it in each case? Are leaders necessary to help groups get along? Give your opinion and an example to support it.

- Folktales often have special endings. What is the most common special ending used in folklore? What special endings are used in these stories?

- These folktales probably originated in Europe and are all variations of the same tale. Which one is your favorite?

# Cooperation Pays Map

*Directions:* Find the continent for each folktale. Choose a colored pencil or fine-tipped marker to color both the continent and the matching box in the legend.

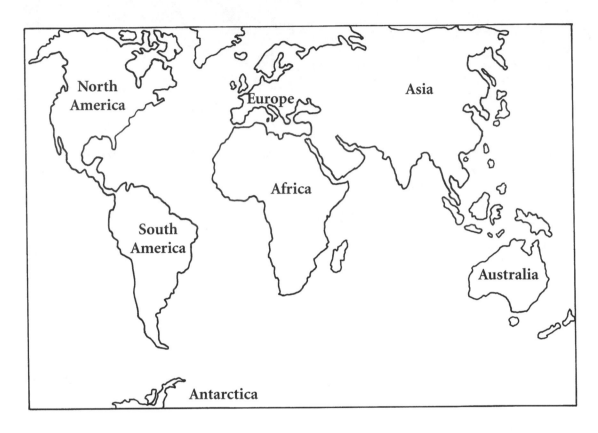

☐ Germany ("The Brementown Musicians")

☐ Ireland ("Jack and the Traveling Animals")

☐ Puerto Rico ("The Traveling Musicians")

☐ Russia ("The Ox and His Animal Friends")

☐ Slovenia ("The Bull and His Animal Friends")

# Animal Collage

*Directions:* Use an 11" × 18" sheet of black construction paper as a background for a collage of any folktale in this unit. Tear brown construction paper for the tree and pieces of green for the leaves. Color and cut out animals from heavy paper and glue onto the collage. Add silver stick-on stars for a final touch.

# Animal Pop-Up

*Directions:* Choose a folktale from the unit to illustrate in a pop-up. Use the three drawings below to guide you in creating the background framework on a sheet of paper. Color the scenery. On a second sheet of paper, draw and color the folktale animals. Then glue the animals onto the background looking into the cottage.

# Letters to the Editor

*Directions:* Letters written to the editor often express opposite views. Here are some ideas for letters:

- It was right/wrong for the animals to run away from their owners.
- It was right/wrong for the animals to take over the robbers' home and belongings.
- It is right/wrong to do away with old, useless animals.

Letter to the Editor
Con

Letter to the Editor
Pro

## Story Wheel

*Directions:* Choose a folktale to present in a story wheel. The pictures appear in the window of the wheel and the words that match are on the outside edge. Practice on scratch paper first so you can present the story in eight sections. You will need a brad and scissors to put the wheel together.

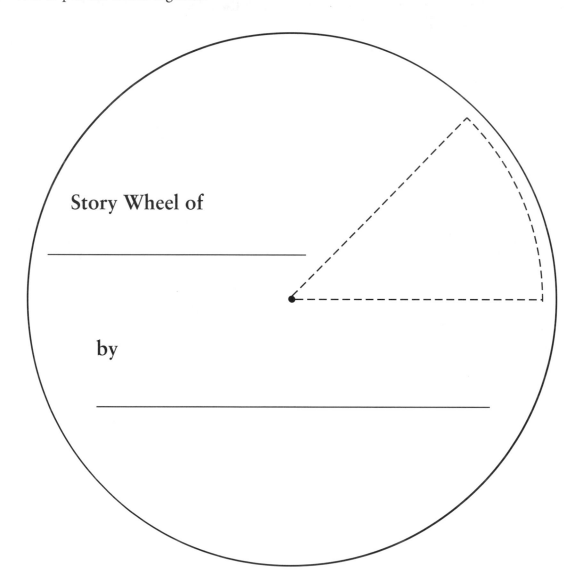

**Story Wheel of**

_____

**by**

_____

continued

## Story Wheel (continued)

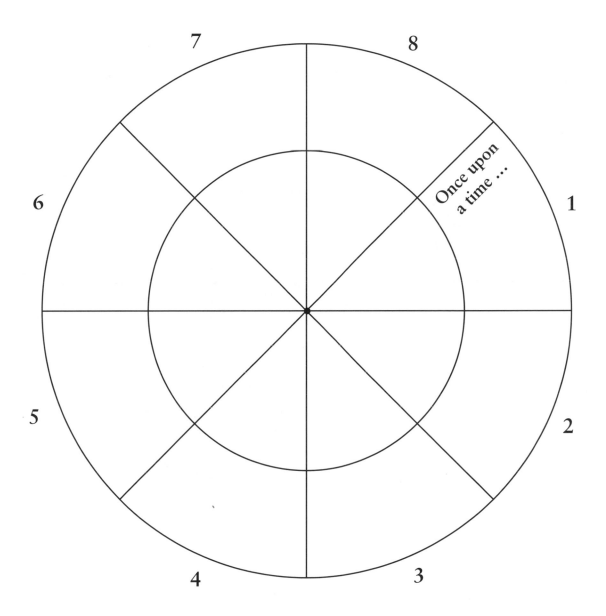

7    8

6    Once upon a time …    1

5    2

4    3

# Bibliography

Grimm, Jacob. *The Bremen Musicians*. New York: Picture Book Studio, 1988.

Picture Book Studio's outstanding book illustrated by Josef Palecek uses a text close to the original Grimm version. The stylized artwork is done in vivid hues, especially bright blue and yellow.

————. *The Bremen Town Musicians*. New York: North-South Books, 1992.

Bernadette Watts illustrated this large, lovely version using an original translation by Anthea Bell.

————. *The Brementown Musicians*. New York: McGraw-Hill, 1968.

Paul Galdone's blue, orange, and gray watercolor version, while an older one, is outstanding. Galdone's special talent—the drawing of lively, big-eyed animals—is put to good use here. The delightful double spread of the robbers gathered around the feast is the most outstanding picture in the book.

————. *The Musicians of Bremen*. New York: Larousse, 1974.

This excellent, older version from Sven Otto is still available in many libraries. The quality here is mainly due to the colorful, lifelike drawings of the animals. The double spread of the animals sleeping under and on the huge tree is so outstanding that it inspired the collage activity in this unit.

Gross, Ruth Belov. *The Bremen-town Musicians*. New York: Scholastic, 1974.

Jack Kent's whimsical illustrations fill this simply-told paperback version.

Page, P. K. *The Traveling Musicians of Bremen*. Boston: Little, Brown, 1991.

This is a contempory version with attractive, spirited illustrations.

Plume, Ilse. *The Bremen-town Musicians*. Garden City, New York: Doubleday, 1980.

Ilse Plume's Caldecott Honor book is filled with lovely, half-spread watercolor paintings. This book should be available in most children's collections because of the Caldecott Award as well as the overall fine quality.

Stevens, Janet. *The Bremen Town Musicians*. New York: Holiday House, 1992.

Huge, wacky animals and ghastly rogues fill the pages of this large picture book with a riot of color and action.

Wilhelm, Hans. *The Bremen Town Musicians*. New York: Scholastic, 1992.

Hans Wilhelm creates a beautiful watercolor version of this story from the town of Bremen where he was born and raised.

Yolen, Jane. *The Musicians of Bremen: A Tale from Germany*. New York: Simon & Schuster, 1996.

Jane Yolen has added an excellent version of this tale with watercolor illustrations by John Segal.

# Chapter 8

# Never Give Up
# (The Cinderella Theme)

## Introduction

This unit can be used successfully by a wide range of ages simply by controlling the number of variants used and selecting the most appropriate activities.

There are many rare variants in this unit to read aloud to students or you can choose from an abundance of beautifully illustrated picture-book variants in the Bibliography to share with children. The bibliography section on pages 170–172 is devoted solely to the many versions of the French "Cinderella," which was retold and published by Charles Perrault in 1697.

The children's publishing industry has shown an avid interest in "Cinderella" variants and parodies in the last few years, providing a huge array of multicultural folktales to enjoy in the study of this unit.

Even a feature film *Ever After*, starring Drew Barrymore and Anjelica Huston (PG-13), is based upon this enduring theme!

### Critical Analysis

Begin this unit by sharing the background information on pages 124–125. Duplicate and distribute copies of the Comparative Checklist on page 157 to give children an effective way to keep track of the elements of all these tales. Each child can fill it out individually or it can be done as a group at the end of each story.

The "Trivia Game" is great fun and works better if questions are composed as the stories are read aloud. This makes a great culminating activity that can be played like a game show with different teams competing for points. The Comparison Checklists can be used by groups that need a little more help to remember the details of the many folktales.

The "Academy Award" activity works well with a wide age range and, like the previous two activities, is easier if filled out as the unit progresses rather than at the end. The directions caution children to use a pencil to mark awards because they may change their minds during the unit.

*Art*

The "Cinderella Pop-Up" is a simple project for younger children or can be made more complex for older children by using larger sheets of paper and adding fabric to create a collage.

Another creative activity for cooperative groups is to construct a nine-square quilt based on each variant as shown below. Each square features a character, setting, magical item, or animal. A title/culture square sits in the center of the quilt. The squares are arranged into a patchwork quilt, mounted on large sheets of colored paper, and hung on walls.

A different art activity involves comparing many of the colorful features of these variants, such as shoes, dresses, jewelry, horses and their equipment, and other animals. For example, children can use larger sheets of paper (12" × 17") to create a shop or museum display of dresses used in the many "Cinderella" variants. Label each dress with the name of girl who wore it and the culture. Larger boxes of crayons include metallic colors, which come in handy for this project.

### Discussion

After hearing a few stories, some students (especially girls) may question the stereotypical goal of securing a husband. That would be a good opportunity to introduce the activity page "Folklore Stereotypes." Older students enter into spirited discussions of all these stereotypes, from the size of feet to more important ideas.

These variants provide a fertile ground for the study of the elements in folklore: special beginnings and endings, repetition, magic, and "threeness" abound in these stories. These elements provide a framework for each story. As soon as the tale begins, the reader can expect certain things: each trial will require three attempts; magic is always an option if the going gets too tough; and good will always triumph over evil. Stop reading at various points to allow children to predict the next turn of the plot based on these folklore elements.

### Writing

The "Lost Ending" is a creative writing activity that allows children to decide how the story ends, or they might enjoy writing and sharing a parody; an extensive bibliography of "Cinderella" parodies can be found on pages 170–172. Obviously, the idea of writing a spoof based on Cinderella is not new, but it is fun each time a new one comes out. Dramatic presentation of the spoofs is an entertaining extension.

### Vocabulary

"Cinderella Crossword" provides an additional culminating activity for individuals or pairs to complete at the end of the study.

# Background Information

 hen you mention Cinderella, most Americans think of Walt Disney's animated version: the fair-skinned teenage girl with upswept blonde hair, pale blue gown with puffed sleeves, and high heels. In fact, this 1951 film became so popular in this country that Cinderella's castle was built as the cornerstone of the Disney theme parks in both California and Florida. Many visitors to the Disney parks may not realize that almost all ethnic groups have their own variant of the ancient tale. Folktale variants of the Cinderella theme are the most widely spread and beloved tales of all time. The story has been found in most cultures throughout the world (more than four hundred variants are known today) and at widely varying times in history.

The first written variant may have been the Egyptian one recorded by a Roman historian in the first century B.C. The written Chinese variant is also quite ancient, dating back to the Tang dynasty, which ruled from 1618 B.C. to 907 A.D. Early variants in Europe include a Scottish one, mentioned as early as 1540, and the Italian variant, "Cenerentola," published in 1634.

In 1697 a Frenchman, Charles Perrault, collected several fairy tales and published them. They were thought to have been stories originally told to his son Pierre by his governess. The variant of "Cinderella" that he used may have been the Italian "Cenerentola." Since Perrault was an elegant French writer and rewrote the fairytale for children of the French royalty, he changed the story considerably by reducing the violence and adding the godmother, pumpkin coach, six horses of dappled mouse gray, and the glass slipper. Perrault's book was very popular in France and was later translated into English and published in London in the early 1700s.

The story was also popular in Germany and was published there by the Brothers Grimm in 1812. Their version contained more of the original violence.

When Walt Disney chose a version to use for the full length feature cartoon, he selected Perrault's elegant French version; consequently, that particular mental image of the tale has been most dominant in this country, leading people to think that the story originated in France.

The terms "Cinderella team" and "Cinderella complex" have become part of our modern language. Perhaps psychologically, most people like to root for the underdog—the good person with disadvantages. That is what the term "Cinderella team" has come to mean—a team with disadvantages in terms of size, skill, or finances that perseveres in the face of overwhelming odds.

Cinderella stories can be positive in that they give hope to individuals enduring trying circumstances. On the other hand, these tales contain many stereotypes which need to be examined and discredited. The "Cinderella complex"—the idea that the main goal of a young woman's life is to marry a wealthy man who will take care of her—is an example of just one stereotype found in these tales. But most importantly, the theme of a young girl never giving up and overcoming great obstacles makes a very appealing, captivating story, or these variants never would have spread so far and survived for so long.

# Polo, the Snake-Girl (Africa—Lesotho)

ome wonderful tales are told about snakes in Basutoland. This is not strange. For there are many of these crawling creatures in that part of Africa's South. There are, indeed, quite as many as there are in the junglelands farther north.

There are small snakes with deadly bites. And there are huge snakes whose fangs do not hold poison at all. The biggest are the pythons, and their cousins, the boas.

Some boas live on the land. Some are at home in the water. And the skin of either kind may be long enough to cover a person from his head to his toes.

Polo was the name by which the Basuto tribe in this ancient tale knew the water boa. And it was a polo's skin that saved the life of their Chief's daughter.

That chief had two wives. They should have lived peacefully with one another, since each had her own hut in the Chief's courtyard. But the Head Wife was jealous. She was a wicked woman, Oh, yes, indeed she was. Each time a baby was born to the Other Wife, she took it away, and no one ever saw it again. She wanted no children but her own in the Chief's courtyard.

"We are to have another child soon," the Other Wife told the Chief one day. "Let me go home to my own father's hut until our baby is born. Perhaps then this one will live." What she really meant was that it would be safer out of the reach of the Head Wife.

Well, the baby was a girl, a beautiful little girl. And the Other Wife was happy. But she also was worried.

"I dare not take my child back to my husband's courtyard," she said to her parents. "She must be kept out of reach of the jealous Head Wife. Let me leave her with you! And let us hide her well so that the wicked woman will not know that she lives."

The grandmother covered the baby up with the skin of a water boa. "Alas, my grandchild is only a polo, for all she has the shape of a girl." This is the way she explained the child in the boa's skin.

Polo was the name by which the little girl was known in the village. No stranger would have guessed that under the brown boa skin there was such a beautiful child.

Only the people in the village where the girl grew up, knew her secret. Her grandparents, in whose hut she lived, loved her well. As she grew bigger they found a larger boa skin to cover her. They cared for her tenderly until she was grown.

Polo's mother was sad that she could not have her dear daughter with her. She was a wife of the Chief. It was her duty to stay in his courtyard. But it would never have been safe to bring Polo into her hut. This Other Wife of the Chief had to content herself with secret visits to the grandparent's hut.

Now the Head Wife, too, had a daughter, Khoa, about the same age as Polo. She was nice-looking, but not nearly so pretty as the girl under the snakeskin. Nor was she as kind. Indeed, Khoa was a good deal like her mother, the wicked Head Wife.

In those days the great hero of that part of Basutoland was the young hunter, Masilo. Wherever he went, people admired him. So there was excitement in the village of this Chief when Masilo appeared there. He was seeking a wife, he said, and he had brought with him his mother who could help him decide whom to marry.

The Chief set aside several huts, one for Masilo, one for his mother, and others for their warrior guards. He made the young hero welcome with a magnificent feast. And when he learned that the young man was wanting a wife, he sent out a call to all the girls in that neighborhood. A day was named when they should present themselves for the choosing.

Secretly, the mother of Polo ran off to tell her dear daughter. The girl was still wearing her ugly boa's skin. Even now, when she was of an age to marry, none but the people in her grandfather's village knew that Polo was a beautiful girl, not the child of a snake.

On the way to meet Masilo, Polo and other girls from that village walked over a road that ran by a river. At one point, as they neared the hero's hut, they came upon Khao, the daughter of the Chief's Head Wife. She was with a group of her own friends. Each of them hoped to be the lucky bride, but they knew it would more likely be the Chief's daughter.

Polo gave Khao greeting. But Khao turned away from her.

I'll have nothing to do with a girl who wears a snake's skin," Khao said scornfully. "A snake-girl would not be a fit bride for an ordinary man, let alone for Masilo. You may just as well go home. He will not want a polo."

Farther along the road, Polo and her friends decided to cool themselves in the river. At the foot of a hillside, they threw off their robes. They little guessed that above them, on the hill, was Masilo himself. He had taken his place there that he might look the girls over, before they came to his hut.

"Who is the girl with the boa's skin?" Masilo pointed to Polo. Amid the other girls, she stood out because of her brown snake covering.

Just then she threw off the serpent's skin. She dived into the water. And Masilo called out again.

"Who is that girl? She is the fairest of any of these young bathers." He was looking at the same time at Khao and her friends who had also decided to cool themselves in the river.

When the girls were lined up next day before Masilo, Khao's group were on one side. Polo and her friends stood on the other. And the tests began.

"Khao, give me a pinch of snuff." Masilo held out his little brass snuffbox. He spoke to her first, according to custom, since she was the Chief's daughter, and her mother was the Head Wife.

This girl was not clever. She poured out far too much snuff into the hero's hand. But he took it just the same, without saying a word.

Then Masilo turned to Polo.

"Give me a pinch of snuff," he asked a second time.

Khao and here friends burst into rude laughter.

"He asks the snake-girl! Oh! Oh!" they tittered behind their hands. They thought it was only a joke.

But Polo quickly took a small pinch from the snuffbox. It was exactly the right amount. And the hero smiled as he thanked her.

"Do you take snuff from the hand of a snake-girl, Masilo?" Khao could not keep her thoughts to herself. And Masilo answered her with a stern voice.

"I will tell you a secret, Daughter of the Head Wife of the chief. Polo is no snake, for all she has a snake's name. Polo, like yourself, is the daughter of the Chief. Those things I discovered when she bathed in the river under my hillside, and when I asked the Chief's Other Wife who she was."

With that, he lifted the boa's skin from the girl.

All in the Chief's courtyard were amazed. None was more surprised that the wicked Head Wife, unless it was the Chief himself. They had been told that the girl baby of the Other Wife had died at birth.

"Give a large bowl of food to Polo," Masilo called to is mother. "Give a small bowl to Khao." This showed, of course, which one he liked best.

Then, with his fingers, Masilo took a bit of the food from Khao's bowl. He could not slight her entirely. But he used his iron spoon and he ate much, much more from the bowl Polo held out to him.

Foolish Khao would still not believe that her rival was not a snake. "Look at Masilo," she cried out. "He eats with a water boa!"

"Cook a fat sheep! We will make a feast for Polo and her friends," Masilo called to his mother. Then he added, "You can cook a small goat for the other ones."

The Head Wife's daughter was angry then.

"He gives a fat sheep to the snake-girl, and only a goat to me!" she screamed. "How is it that you make such a fine feast for a snake?"

Masilo did not answer. And when the night came, he paid a short visit of politeness to the hut where Khao was. He soon left to seek Polo, and he spent the whole evening with her and her friends.

"Take off that ugly serpent's skin, Polo," he said as they sat together on the mat inside her hut.

"The skin has protected me," the girl answered. "It has kept me safe. I am accustomed to wear it."

"You no longer need it. I choose you for my bride. You shall be my Head Wife. And never again shall you hide under the boa's skin." He tore the brown snakeskin to pieces, and he burned them up in the fire.

"Mother, we have work to do this day," he said the next morning. "My men shall lay a path of clean mats on the ground from your hut to mine. Prepare the wedding banquet. I shall wed Polo this day." His mother nodded. She was pleased with his choice.

Khao and her friends watched what went on with heavy hearts. They were not sure just what all the preparations were about, but they were uneasy in their minds.

Masilo's warriors decorated their buffalo-hide shields with long, waving ostrich plumes. They then lined themselves up on each side of the mat-covered walkway from the mother's hut to Masilo's. And they held their plumed shields up so that they made a shady arch over the path.

"Come forth, Polo, my bride!" the young man called to the girl who had been taken into the hut of his mother.

When Polo stepped forth, it was as if her shining beauty made the sun pale for a moment. When it burst forth again, the copper rings on her arms and legs shone bright as gold. Tall and lovely, she walked under the arch of war shields to the hut of the bridegroom.

It was then that the Chief and his two wives, and all the village saw Polo married to Masilo. They cheered and they wished them well, and all said Polo was the most beautiful bride in the land.

Only Khao was unhappy. Until that moment, she had not believed it could happen. Only then did she remember that this snake-girl, like herself, was a daughter of the Chief. Now she cried out in her disappointment. She sobbed and she moaned. And Masilo took pity on her.

"Do not cry, Khao. You shall be my Other Wife, if Polo consents. Polo shall always walk first, for she is my Head Wife. You shall wait upon her. You shall obey her commands. But we will be kind to you."

And that is how it turned out. It was an honor to be any one of the wives of a hero like Masilo. Khao looked quickly to see whether the girl she had scorned would give her consent. But Polo was good and kind. She smiled at this girl who was to be her husband's Other Wife.

Masilo brought one hundred cows and two hundred sheep to pay for his two brides. Then his men formed a close circle about Polo. Under the shade of their plumed shields, she walked off behind her hero husband to his own village.

Khao came behind them. As is the lot of the Other Wife, she carried a bundle upon her head. Poor Khao! To the end of her days she was the servant of the snake-girl.

# The Princess and the Sea Serpent (Brazil)

nce upon a time a young princess lived in a splendid royal palace. Surrounding the palace were many beautiful gardens filled with lovely flowers, lush green plants, and bright-colored birds of all kinds. The princess's favorite part of the gardens was one section that sloped down to the ocean. The little girl loved to sit on a bench and watch the changes in the glimmering blue sea.

The princess seemed to have everything a girl could want, yet she was very lonely, as she had no brothers or sisters or friends to play with.

One morning as she sat watching the sparkling sunlight dance on the tops of the waves, she cried out, "I am so lonely! If only I had someone to play with me!"

Suddenly, out of a huge breaker a large sea serpent arose, wriggled in the air, and came up on shore. At first the princess was frightened, but the sea serpent quickly reassured her in a comforting voice, "Do not be afraid, little girl, for I hear your distress, and I have come to be your playmate."

The serpent was kind, as well as magical, and helped to fill the lonely girl's days with laughter and fun.

Days grew into years and finally the princess was sixteen, a young woman of marriageable age.

The sea serpent, too, had grown older and one day sadly said to the princess, "Our days of play by the ocean are gone now. Though I will no longer come out of the water to be with you each day, I will always be your friend. If ever you should need help, only call out my name to the waves and I will come to your rescue."

With that, the serpent silently and swiftly disappeared into the foam at the edge of the sea. Not long after, the queen of a neighboring kingdom lay on her deathbed.

She implored her husband the king, "Here is my ring. When you wish to remarry, choose only a bride whose finger fits this ring perfectly."

After a period of mourning, the old king set forth to the homes of young maidens to have them try on the ring. For some the ring was too loose. For others the ring was so tight they could not push it onto their fingers. At last the king came to the palace of the princess. To her father's delight, the princess's finger fit into the ring perfectly. The old king ruled a very large and wealthy kingdom, so the the princess's father was overjoyed at the alliance. But the princess had hoped in her heart to wed a young and handsome prince, not an old, unattractive king.

One evening as the princess sat weeping on her bench near the ocean, she remembered the promise made to her by her old friend the sea serpent. So she walked down to the edge of the water and softly called out to the serpent.

The serpent rose out of the water, just as she had in the past and asked the girl to tell her of her problems. The princess quickly explained that she was soon to marry the old king.

"Fear not," replied the sea serpent. "Go back and send word to the old king that you will marry him as soon as he gives you a dress the color of all the flowers in the forest."

This was a difficult request, but the old king was able to fulfill it, and so the princess was once again at the ocean's edge seeking help from her serpentine friend.

"Fear not," comforted the sea serpent. "This time send word that you will marry the old king as soon as he gives you a dress the color of all the fish in the ocean."

This request was even more difficult, but once again the old king sent the fabulous dress to the princess, and she again fled to the sea for advice.

"This time, tell the old king that this will be your last request, but you absolutely must have a dress the color of the sky and all the stars within it," counseled the sea serpent.

The old king was nearly overwhelmed by this last request, but finally he was able to fulfill it and sent the dress to the palace along with a final wedding date.

This time when the princess called her friend from the ocean, the serpent told her, "Gather your three dresses and meet me here at the edge of the ocean at dusk."

The princess did as she was told and was astounded at the strange little boat that awaited her at the water's edge.

"This little magic boat will carry you away to another land where lives a very charming, handsome prince," explained the sea serpent.

"What a wonderful friend you have been to me!" explained the princess. "What can I do to thank you for your great kindnesses?"

"There is one, very important thing that you can do for me," answered the sea serpent, "On the day of your marriage to the prince, you can call my name three times and the magic spell will be broken that keeps me in the form of a serpent rather than a lovely princess like yourself."

The princess readily agreed and assured her friend that she would never forget her. With that, she boarded the little ship with her box of three dresses and set sail for a long voyage.

Finally she reached the shore of a lovely land, and as she walked onto the beach with her box of dresses, the little ship magically disappeared.

The princess soon realized that she would need to work for her food and lodging, so she went to all the fine houses, asking for employment. Because she had always lived a leisurely life as a princess, she was qualified to do only the most lowly of tasks, that of tending the chickens. It was a hard life for the girl, but she only had to think of the aging king to be satisfied with her lot.

After some time had passed, a great fiesta was to be held in the land. All in the great house except the chicken girl made careful preparations to attend. After the others left, the chicken girl cleaned herself and put on the dress that was the color of all the flowers in the forest.

The prince of the land, who was young and dashing, immediately noticed the lovely young maiden in the colorful gown. No one in the land knew who the girl was, but they all admired her grace and beauty. She left the fiesta early and was back at the great house tending the chickens before the household returned.

The second day of the fiesta went as before, only this time the chicken girl wore the dress that was the color of all the fish in the ocean.

The prince was frustrated at not being able to discover the maiden's name or home, but decided that he would marry her.

The third day of the fiesta went as before, with the chicken girl wearing her dress that was the color of the sky and all the stars within it. This time, just before she slipped away from him, the prince gave the maiden a rare jewel.

Time passed and the prince despaired of ever seeing his beloved again. The young man lost his appetite and became sickly and thin. Throughout the land, young maidens prepared tempting dishes to appeal to the prince and win his approval.

Finally the chicken girl came to the palace with a bowl of soup in which she had dropped the precious jewel. The prince took a taste of the soup and was about to send it away, when he noticed the jewel in the bottom.

"Who prepared this soup?" he asked his mother, the queen.

"I believe it was the chicken girl," she replied.

The girl, who had already changed into her dress that was the color of the sky and all the stars within it, was immediately brought to him, and they were both filled with joy as the prince set the wedding feast for the very next day.

But alas, the princess was so overjoyed on her wedding day that she completely forgot the request of her friend, the sea serpent. So the evil magic spell was not broken, and the poor girl was resigned to live forever in the form of a sea serpent.

That is why, even today, when you stand quietly near the sea, you can hear the soft moaning of the sea serpent who was forgotten by the one she had helped so greatly.

# Trembling (Ireland)

Long ago an Irish nobleman had three daughters, named Fair, Brown, and Trembling. Lovely though they all were, the youngest daughter was by far the most beautiful.

The older two were always concerned with adorning themselves in fine clothing and attracting the attention of the marriageable young nobles. For that reason they would not allow the youngest to leave the house, not even for Mass on Sunday, for they so feared that Trembling's beauty would bring her a marriage proposal before them.

One Sunday morning after Fair and Brown had left for Mass in their finest garments, Trembling was working in the kitchen, preparing a hearty meal for her family to eat after Mass.

"And why are you at home when it's at church you ought to be on a Sunday morning?" inquired the old hen woman, who had smelled bannock baking and trooped into the noble kitchen to investigate.

"And how could I attend, in me tattered clothes, and me sisters not wanting me to be seen outside these walls?" answered Trembling indignantly.

"'Twill not be a worry," assured the old hen woman confidently. "Only tell me your choice for a fine gown to wear to Mass."

With that the young girl pondered just a moment and then said, "Very well, I would like a gown as white as a shamrock's flower with shoes as green as a shamrock's leaves."

The old hen woman swirled her ancient, decrepit cape about her and pulled out not only the requested garments, but also soft, white leather gloves. When Trembling was dressed and ready to leave, the hen woman opened the front door to reveal a beautiful white mare with a golden saddle and bridle for Trembling to ride to the church.

When the girl was mounted, the old hen woman warned her, "Now mind you, do not go into the church, and when the people rise at the end of the Mass, race away for home as fast as the mare can run."

All during the Mass people strove to peek out the open door of the church at the stunning stranger sitting atop a white mare. At the end of the service everyone, especially the young men, scurried outside the church to meet the young maiden. But there was no one in the churchyard for the white mare was swift as the stormy sea wind.

When Fair and Brown returned from Mass, Trembling was once again in her old rags tending the midday meal.

"And do you carry any news from church today?" the youngest daughter asked innocently.

"Aye, we do," answered Fair excitedly. "There was a grand lady astride a fine white mare that watched Mass from outside the front door."

"She put our gowns to shame," added Brown, "and turned the head of every man in the church. We must have new gowns made for next Sunday in the same style and color."

The following Sunday saw the same events. Fair and Brown left for Mass in their new white gowns and Trembling started the midday meal as usual. The hen woman again appeared in the kitchen and again requested Trembling's choice of garments for church.

This time Trembling said, "Fine black satin as shiny as a crow's wing would be grand for a gown, with shoes as red as summer's first rose."

Once again the hen woman swirled her cape about and produced the magnificent garments for Trembling. Only this time the mare was jet black and glossy with a shining saddle fashioned of the finest silver.

Again when Trembling left for the church, the old hen woman gave her the same admonition to stay outside the church and return when the parishioners stood up at the end.

All went as before, and when the older sisters returned from church for their dinner, they could scarcely eat for talking about the strange visitor at Mass.

"It was little the men looked at our new gowns, for their mouths were all gaping open at the sight of the noble lady outside the church," said Fair.

"Aye, and new black gowns we must have for next Sunday's Mass," added Brown.

The following Sunday the older sisters were no sooner out of the house in their new black gowns than the hen woman was once more at the kitchen door to talk with Trembling.

"What sort of a gown would you fancy this week?" she asked the joyous girl.

"One that has a skirt as red as the first rose of summer, and a blouse as white as a shamrock's flower, and a cape as green as a shamrock's leaves with shoes as black as a crow's wing."

This time the mare waiting in the courtyard to speed the girl to church was white with golden colored spots and a golden saddle and bridle.

Everything went as before, only this time the Prince of Ireland, who had heard of the noblewoman's beauty and wealth, was stationed behind a thicket near the church door. When Trembling raced away from the church on her mare, the prince swiftly pursued her on his stallion, nearly catching her. He was able only to grab her shoe before the mare outdistanced the stallion.

When Trembling returned home, she was very upset that she had lost her shoe to the prince and thought the hen woman would be angry.

"Don't fret," said the old woman. "It will all be for the best."

This time when the older sisters returned home, they told Trembling that the prince was going to search all of Ireland to find the owner of the shoe, whom he considered the most beautiful young maiden to ever grace the isle. Determined, the prince set forth to have each young maiden in Ireland try on the shoe until he found the one that it fit.

Now the shoe was of a common size, being neither large nor small, but it never quite fit any girl's foot though many tried with a vengeance. Finally the prince's entourage neared the nobleman's residence. Fair and Brown were filled with excitement at the prospect of trying on the shoe.

Then Trembling piped up, "Maybe it's my foot that the shoe with fit."

At that the older sisters hooted and laughed and finally shut the younger girl into a closet so she would not be an embarrassment to them in her rags.

Though the older sisters tried and tried, the shoe would not fit either of them. Just as the prince's entourage was leaving, Trembling cried through the door of the closet, "Please let me try the shoe!"

Over the sister's protests, the men released Trembling from the closet and bade her try on the shoe.

As the prince looked up from her foot into her face, he said, "Of course, you are the young maiden that I pursued. I want you for my wife."

Trembling asked the prince to excuse her for a short time, while she dashed from the room to the hen woman's hovel where the old woman once again outfitted her in stunning attire. The prince beamed at her loveliness when she returned, but alas, word soon arrived that other princes of the realm wanted to fight the prince for the hand of the maiden.

Each day for a week the prince successfully fought with his sword yet another adversary. At the end of that time, all other suitors bowed out and the prince was free to marry Trembling.

They had many, many children and lived until they were both quite old.

# Cenerentola (Italy)

nce upon a time there lived a prince whose wife died leaving him with a young daughter. Although cherished by her grieving father, the little girl came to love the governess he had hired to care for her.

One day the girl wistfully said to the governess, "You are so good to me, I wish you were my mother."

"But you could become my dear little girl, if only you will do as I tell you," advised the crafty governess. "Whenever you talk privately with your father, tell him of my virtues and beseech him to marry me."

So the child did as she was advised, extolling the woman's virtues and so proclaiming her love for the governess that the prince finally relented and married the woman.

During the wedding celebration the girl was standing near a window when a small white dove suddenly flew in and settled softly on her shoulder.

Before she could brush it away, the dove quickly whispered in her ear, "What ever you need, merely send me your request and it shall be done."

With that the dove swiftly flew away, leaving the girl astonished, but delighted.

For some time the stepmother treated her with great love and kindness. Then one day the stepmother revealed that, rather than the unmarried governess they had thought her to be, she was actually a widow with several daughters of her own. She soon brought them to the palace where they, along with their mother, so bedazzled the prince that he forgot about his own daughter. Even worse, the stepmother falsely maligned the girl to her father so that she was banished to the kitchen where she became known as Cenerentola (which means Cinderella).

Soon a great feast was to be held in the village. The stepmother and stepsisters worked for days to perfect their dazzling attire. In despair Cenerentola went to the window, closed her eyes, and uttered the magic chant which the dove had taught her. Suddenly she was dressed in beautiful, elegant clothes, seated upon a magnificent horse, and accompanied by attendants in stunning array.

Attending the feast was the young king himself. When he saw the exquisite Cenerentola, he was enchanted. He immediately ordered his manservant to follow Cenerentola home after the party to discover who she was and where she lived.

When Cenerentola noticed the servant following her, she threw a handful of gold coins to the ground, distracting him long enough for her to return home and change clothes. The young king was furious to have lost every trace of the lovely maiden and vowed to better pursue her at the next celebration.

Soon another celebration was announced to the villagers. Again, the young king planned to attend as did the stepmother and stepsisters. And again Cenerentola went to the window and called to the magic dove and so was able to attend the feast in grandeur.

This time, though, the king's manservant, under threat of death, followed the girl very closely after the gala. Cenerentola's coachman took off at such high speed to elude the king's manservant that the maiden lost one of her beautiful slippers. The frustrated king, upon receiving word of the lost girl and a single slipper, quickly announced a great feast. All the women of the kingdom were summoned to attend in order to discover the owner of the slipper.

When all the women of the realm were assembled, the king inquired of the crowd, "Does anyone know of a young woman not in attendance here tonight?"

The prince felt obligated to admit to the king that he had a daughter at home, but she had become such a slovenly, disgraceful girl that the fair maiden could not possibly be her. The king immediately demanded that the girl be brought to the banquet before the search began for the owner of the missing slipper. When the king saw Cenerentola, he glanced at her strangely but said nothing.

One by one the women tried on the tiny slipper, all to no avail. Lastly the slipper came to Cenerentola, where it slipped onto her delicate foot as if by magic. The young king swept Cenerentola into his arms and declared her queen of his kingdom.

# Kongjee (Korea)

ong, long ago there lived a couple who dearly wished for a child, but had not been blessed with one. At last their prayers were answered and a beautiful baby girl, whom they named Kongjee, was born. Their hearts were filled with joy, for the child was as good and kind as she was beautiful.

But alas! Their good fortune was not to last. One day the young mother fell ill and died soon after. The father and Kongjee grieved and grieved. As Kongjee grew older, she learned to cook and clean for their little family and they managed together for several years. The father, though, noted silently that Kongjee's hair and clothes were never quite as smooth and stylish as when the mother had been there to tend her precious daughter.

The father also began to think about his own future. In a few years Kongjee would marry and then he would need a wife. He decided that remarrying would solve both problems: Kongjee would have a mother to help her and he would have a wife to care for him in the years to come.

A perfect solution seemed to be in the widow and her daughter Potjee who lived in the village. The father was delighted as Potgee was about the same age as Kongjee.

"Sisters to laugh and play and work together!" thought the man.

But it was not to be. From the very beginning Potjee and her mother were jealous of Kongjee's beauty and gentle ways. Soon Kongjee was working from early morning to late at night doing all the work in the household and most of the work on the small farm. To make matters worse, Potjee and her mother called Kongjee a filthy pig because she grew soiled from the dirty labor.

The time came when the rice fields needed to be hoed and cleared for planting. Naturally, the stepmother told Kongjee to do this task while she and Potjee went to the market to admire the goods and shop.

"If you don't have the fields cleared by the time we return, you shall be beaten and receive no supper," declared the cruel stepmother.

Poor Kongjee stood dejectedly before the rocky fields with her hoe in her hand and tears streaming down her face. How could she ever complete the backbreaking task in time?

Suddenly a gentle breeze whipped across the fields and a huge magical black ox appeared before the weeping girl.

"Why do you cry so sorrowfully?" asked the beast sympathetically.

"I must clear this field before evening or I will be beaten and have no supper to eat," answered the heartbroken girl.

"This will not be difficult to do," said the ox as he calmly, but quickly, used his teeth and massive jaw to uproot and clear the field of weeds and rocks.

When the stepmother and Potjee arrived home, they found an excited Kongjee waiting for them. She held a basket of shiny apples under her arm.

"How did you ever complete that task?" shouted the enraged woman. "Did you steal those apples?"

"No, they were given to me by a kind ox who cleared the field," answered Kongjee.

"That is a lie!" roared the woman, who snatched the basket of fruit from the girl. "You shall have no supper tonight for lying!"

One of Kongjee's many chores was to carry water from a well to fill a huge water jar by the kitchen door. The jar had developed a hole in the bottom so that every time Kongjee filled it with water, it leaked out. Kongjee grew discouraged with hauling the heavy buckets of water only to have the water seep away.

Again, a small gust of wind blew into the courtyard and a magical toad appeared.

"You will never fill that water jar," said the toad, "but I can help."

The astonished Kongjee replied, "I know that the hole is the problem, but when I tell my stepmother, she blames me and hits me."

"This will not be difficult to do," replied the toad as he leaped into the large jar and used his body to block the hole.

Kongjee did not mention the magic toad, but quickly filled the water jar and went on about her other tasks. Her stepmother, however, knew that there was a hole in the water jar and had used the task as an excuse to hit the girl. When she saw that the jar was filled, she suspected magic and so she said nothing.

One day the family was invited to attend a huge, elegant wedding. Many young men would be attending this gala. The stepmother did not want the lovely Kongjee to outshine her Potjee as both of the girls were of marriageable age.

As they were about to leave for the wedding, the stepmother called Kongjee aside and told her that the rest of the family would go on ahead and she could come as soon as she polished all the rice in two large bags. The stepmother told Kongjee's father that

Kongjee needed to dress her hair better so that she would not disgrace the family and would catch up with them soon.

Kongjee spread the rice out on straw mats to dry and process and then sat down and began to weep. The task would take hours to complete and she would miss the long-awaited day!

Suddenly, a gust of wind blew a flock of small birds into the courtyard where they landed on the rice and quickly hulled and polished it.

"A thousand thanks!" exclaimed the amazed girl to the little birds as they flew off into the sky.

Kongjee wiped her eyes, smoothed her hair, and merrily set forth for the wedding feast.

She had not walked too far, however, before she heard flag bearers shouting, "Make way! Make way!"

Behind them came a nobleman being carried in an ornately decorated palanquin.

Kongjee quickly jumped aside and bowed her head as the palanquin moved by. Because she moved so rapidly, her straw sandal fell off and rolled down a small embankment into a tiny stream.

The nobleman shouted for the palanquin bearers to stop so he could help the girl retrieve her sandal. But Kongjee became frightened and sped away. Watching her run, the nobleman was struck by her beauty. He ordered his men to retrieve the sandal from the stream and they continued on their way to attend a wedding.

When Kongjee arrived, her stepmother was angry because she was certain that Kongjee would never be able to attend the wedding. The other guests were delighted to see the kind and lovely girl. Though they wondered why she came to the wedding with only one shoe, no one mentioned it; they knew her life was harsh, living with a hard-hearted stepsister and stepmother.

At last the nobleman and his men arrived at the wedding. Hoping to find the owner of the sandal, the nobleman asked the guests if they knew who owned a straw sandal to match the one in his hand.

"It's my daughter's!" shouted the stepmother as she rushed up with Potjee in hand and grabbed the sandal from the nobleman.

Potjee sat down and tried to cram her big foot into the tiny shoe, much to the guests' amusement. Finally, the nobleman's assistant brusquely stopped this charade and told the women to leave.

Then, an elderly and dignified guest said to the nobleman, "There is a young woman here who is too well behaved to call attention to herself, but I think you will see that she is missing a sandal much like that one."

At that Kongjee was brought forward where she gently slid her tiny foot into the sandal. The nobleman invited her to sit next to him during the wedding feast, where he fell in love with her good sense and kind heart, not to mention her beauty. At the end of the celebration he asked to see Kongjee's father.

"Sir, would you kindly allow your daughter to marry me?" asked the nobleman graciously. "She is everything I could want in a noble wife."

Kongjee's father quickly agreed and the couple was soon married in a magnificent ceremony. They had many children and lived in respect and love.

Living with her stepmother and stepsister over the years, Kongjee had learned to be patient, hardworking, and kind. These traits helped her to become a wise ruler; they should be remembered and followed by us to this day.

# Kari Woodendress (Norway)

 There once was a king whose wife died leaving him with a young daughter who was as wise and kind as she was beautiful. The king long grieved for his wife, but eventually grew lonely and married a woman who had a daughter the same age as his own. The stepmother and stepsister were very jealous of the princess for they were as wicked and homely as the princess was fair. The pair hid their hatred and envy of the girl until the king left to lead his army in war and no one was left to protect the princess.

The stepmother cruelly beat the princess, sent her out into the fields to herd the cattle all day, and finally tried to starve her to death.

One day as the thin, hungry girl stood forlornly in the pasture with the animals, a huge bull came over to her and spoke, "I know that the wicked queen has nearly starved you to death, but fret not, my little princess, for I can help you."

The princess was amazed at hearing the bull speak, but continued to listen and follow his directions.

"Reach inside my left ear and pull out a cloth. Spread it on the ground and it will be filled with delicious food," directed the huge bull.

The girl was at first hesitant to get so close to the massive animal, but he seemed so kind and she was so hungry that at last she did as he bid her. To her surprise the cloth was instantly filled with every sort of rich delicacy which the girl greatly enjoyed. Before long the princess was once again rosy and healthy.

When the queen realized that her plan to kill the girl had failed, she ordered her servant to follow the princess and discover the secret of her nourishment. By this time the king had returned home, so the queen resorted to cunning to destroy her step-daughter. She pretended that she had a terrible illness and bribed a doctor to say that only the flesh of the great bull could save her life. When the princess realized that the bull was soon to be killed, she ran sobbing to the field to warn him.

The bull thought a bit and then said, "Soon your father will leave again and, with me dead, you will die soon thereafter. Therefore, we must both flee tonight."

"But I do not want to leave my father without his blessing," cried the princess. "I love him so."

The bull convinced the girl that this was the only way. So, late that night the girl came down to the pasture and secretly fled, riding on the back of the big animal.

The next day the king was notified of the absence of both his daughter and the bull, never thinking of the two of them together. He sent messengers all over the realm to locate the girl, sorrowing when no trace of her could be found.

The bull and the princess traveled far and wide until they came upon a magnificent forest filled entirely with copper trees, copper flowers, and copper grass.

"Be very careful when we go through this forest to not tear loose a leaf or even a blade of grass. A terrible troll with three heads lives here and it will not go well for us if anything is harmed," warned the bull.

"I shall be quite careful," promised the princess.

But alas, the forest was very thick and the unfortunate girl accidentally tore off a copper leaf."

They soon arrived at the edge of the forest where the bull fought a ferocious battle, barely defeating the troll.

After a rest to recover, the two traveled on this time encountering a silver forest. Again the bull cautioned the girl to harm nothing and, again, the girl accidentally pulled off a silver leaf, causing a great battle for the bull and a six-headed troll. It required a long rest and magic potion from the dead troll to help the bull recover, but finally the two went on.

Once again they encountered an amazing, magical forest, this one of gold. As before, the bull warned the girl to damage nothing and, as before, she inadvertently broke off a golden apple. The princess was filled with anguish, as was the bull, but he told her to keep the apple, and he steeled himself for another intense battle. This time the troll was a nine-headed one and nearly defeated the valiant bull. After more magic potion and a much longer rest, the two set off on the final leg of their journey. At last they arrived at a lovely castle near an alpine village.

"Here is where we part," said the brave and magnificent animal. "You will need to go to the pigsty near the castle where you will find a dress made of wood. Put it on and then go to the castle, telling them that you are Kari Woodendress and that you wish a job working in the kitchen."

The princess agreed to do this and was about to ask the bull about his plans, when he suddenly turned to her and said, "This last is most difficult, but it must be done."

"What is it, dear friend?" asked the girl, as she stroked the bull's massive back.

"You must kill me with your knife and cut off my head. Bury it along with the copper leaf, the silver leaf, and the golden apple under this large rock." said the bull. "Then whenever you need me, you have only to touch the rock and make your wish, and I will grant you your every wish."

At first the girl shrieked and cried and refused, but the bull made her understand that this was their only recourse. Finally, she carried out the bloody deed with great sorrow in her heart.

The next morning she appeared at the castle entrance in her wooden dress. She was hired, but only for the most lowly tasks, and she soon grew filthy in her strange wooden clothing.

One day royalty came to the palace and Kari begged to take the fresh bath water to the prince. The other servants thought better of it, but eventually allowed her to do the heavy chore. But the prince was so disgusted at the sight of the dirty girl that he threw the bath water at her.

The following Sunday Kari Woodendress wanted to go to church in the village, so she went to the rock and asked for a decent dress to wear. Magically, a brilliant blue gown adorned with copper ornaments appeared on the rock. While Kari was putting it on, a majestic white horse with a copper saddle and bridle materialized to transport her to church. The prince also attended church in the village that Sunday and instantly fell in love with the lovely maiden in copper and blue.

That night Kari asked to take the clean towels to the prince. Again he threw them at her, calling Kari a filthy troll.

The next Sunday Kari Woodendress wanted to go to church and went again to the rock. This time she received a stunning white gown embroidered elaborately with silver thread, accompanied by a splendid horse of dapple gray with a silver bridle and saddle. The prince fell even more deeply in love with the regal princess but could not discover her name.

Again that evening Kari asked to take clean combs to the prince and, though the other servants thought it a waste, they allowed her to do this chore. Once again the prince flung the combs at her, ordering her out of his sight.

Kari sought to attend church the next Sunday also, so she once again returned to the rock. The elegant gown this time was made entirely of golden thread and encrusted with diamonds. Accordingly, an impressive jet black horse appeared with a golden saddle and bridle.

This time when Kari Woodendress went to church, none of the villagers paid the slightest attention to the sermon for they were all staring at Kari and wondering where she had come from.

The prince determined to have the beauty as his bride and ordered a bucket of tar to be poured in the entrance of the church to trap her. Instead, it only caught her shoe as she raced away from the church.

Maidens throughout the land came to the castle to try on the shoe. It fit none until Kari's stepsister came to the castle. Since it seemed to fit her, the prince had no choice but to marry her though he was loathe to marry a girl so ugly and disagreeable.

While watching the royal wedding party on their way to the church, a villager noticed that blood was dripping from the bride's shoe and called out to the royal couple. At that, the prince stopped the procession and pulled off the golden shoe only to discover that the stepsister had cut off part of her foot to fit into the shoe.

By this time nearly every maiden in the countryside had tried on the golden shoe. "Are there no others?" asked the dismayed prince.

"Only Kari Woodendress," laughed one of the servants, "but, of course, it couldn't be her because she has the feet of a mule."

"Nevertheless, we shall let her attempt, because I decreed that all maidens should try," said the prince, so the poor girl was summoned.

Dirty Kari Woodendress came eagerly clattering into the room in her blackened dress of wood. As she placed her foot into the golden shoe, her miserable wooden covering was instantly transformed into the gleaming golden gown of the previous Sunday. Then all looked down and saw that she was wearing the mate to the golden shoe.

The prince was delighted and even more thrilled when he learned that Kari was a princess. He immediately ordered a lavish wedding celebration.

# Little Burnt Face (United States— Algonquin Indian)

ong ago in a village near the great waters there lived an old chief with three daughters. His wife had died many winters before. The youngest was very gentle, kind, and beautiful. Because the people of the tribe spoke so highly of the youngest sister, the older sisters became very jealous of her and tried to destroy her beauty. They gave her only the filthiest old rags to wear, cut off her long, lovely hair, and, worst of all, scarred her pretty face with coals from the fire. Then they mocked her, calling her Little Burnt Face and telling their father, the old chief, that Little Burnt Face had done these things to herself.

Little Burnt Face kept her songs within her heart and her head bent over her work hoping that her diligent effort would melt the ice within her older sisters' hearts. But nothing could soften their hard ways.

Then one day the sisters' thoughts flew away from their hatred of Little Burnt Face. Many maidens desired the Great Wind as a husband, for he was both very powerful and very gentle. His sister, who dwelt among the People, was helping him in his quest. To find a truthful bride, the Great Wind and his sister devised a clever test. Each evening near sundown the sister took a prospective maiden for a walk along the water's edge. As the Great Wind came home from his day's work, his sister would ask the maiden if she could see him.

Since the Great Wind would only marry a girl who could see him, each maiden would answer, "Yes, of course, I see him."

Then the Great Wind's sister would ask, "And with what does he pull his sled across the sky?"

Each girl would answer, "With a cord made of moose hide or deer hide or vines."

The sister and her brother, the Great Wind, would know that each maiden was lying, for none of those guesses was true.

Eventually, all the maidens of the tribe except Little Burnt Face had tried and lost the trial to become the bride of the the Great Wind. The Great Wind's sister then kindly came to Little Burnt Face and asked if she would undertake the trial to win the hand of the Great Wind.

Little Burnt Face eagerly agreed and carefully cleaned herself and tried to make her rags look as presentable as possible for the trial. Her older sisters laughed at her, for how could someone so ragged and ugly hope to succeed where they had failed?

Villagers snickered behind their hands as they watched the Great Wind's sister and Little Burnt Face set forth for the water. Twilight was descending upon the face of the land as the pair neared the water's edge. Suddenly the sister raised her hand and stopped.

"Do you see him?" she asked.

Little Burnt Face looked about very carefully and then replied softly, with sad resignation, "No, I don't."

A gust of wind then whipped along the shoreline and the sister knew her brother was pleased with the honesty of the girl.

So again she asked, "Now do you see my brother, the Great Wind?"

This time Little Burnt Face beamed and answered with laughter in her voice, "Yes, he is there above the water, pulling his sled."

"What does he use to draw his sled across the sky?"

"The rainbow of many colors."

With that the sister hugged and kissed Little Burnt Face, knowing that at last her brother had found a worthy bride.

Then she took Little Burnt Face home to her own tepee where she bathed the girl's poor burned face, magically restoring it to its original beauty. Suddenly also, Little

Burnt Face's hair grew back in as black and glossy as a raven's wing. Then the sister gave her a beautiful soft white deerskin wedding garment, complete with leggings and moccasins, all richly decorated with many ornaments.

At last the sister stood back and looked upon Little Burnt Face, very pleased with the appearance of the radiant and magnificently attired bride. Then she turned and quickly left the tepee.

Soon the Great Wind entered through the flap in the tepee and became the husband of Little Burnt Face.

The Great Wind, knowing the cruelty that resided in the hearts of Little Burnt Face's older sisters, decided to punish them. He changed them both into aspen trees. Since that time, the leaves of the the aspen always quake when the wind flows near them, because they know that the wind remembers their dishonesty and cruelty to their younger sister so long ago.

# Turkey Girl (United States–Zuni Indian)

Long ago the ancient Zuni Indians had large flocks of turkeys which were tended either by slaves or the lowest levels of their own people. Each day the flocks were taken from their cages and herded onto the hot mesas to forage for food among the piñon, sagebrush, and juniper shrubs.

One such turkey herder was a very poor girl, dressed in the most ragged clothing and yet possessing a pleasing look and manner. Though she received little kindness in life, Turkey Girl nevertheless treated her turkey flock with compassion as she tended them each day. In turn the turkeys all responded obediently to her every call.

One day as Turkey Girl was herding her flock through the canyon, she overheard a priest announce an annual harvest festival of feasting and dancing to be held in a few days.

Being so poor and ill clad, Turkey Girl had never been allowed to even watch these festivities, let alone participate, and she lamented to her turkeys how much she longed to be a part of the festival. Each day as the festival neared, she told the turkeys about the fine food being prepared and the magnificent garments being readied by the villagers.

While resting under a stand of canyon cottonwoods in the late afternoon of the festival day, Turkey Girl was startled when suddenly all the turkeys stopped moving and turned to her at once. The largest gobbler waddled to the front of the flock, fanned out his impressive tail feathers and began to speak importantly, "We have sympathized with you these past few days and feel that you are as worthy to attend this festival as any Zuni in the village.

Turkey Girl was truly astounded, for she had no idea that the turkeys were either listening to her or could speak.

"Listen carefully now," continued the old gobbler. "Would you like to attend this evening to feast and dance with the other young people?"

"You know that I long with all my heart to be a part of the festival!" she replied with laughter and amazement.

"We know your longings," continued the gobbler seriously. "But will you follow our guidance and remember not to treat others as you have been treated?"

Turkey Girl immediately promised to obey the turkeys, just as they had always obeyed her, and to always remember her humble station in life.

Near sundown the turkeys headed back to their cages with their lighthearted herder skipping along beside them. When they reached the cages, the old gobbler told the girl to enter and remove her ragged garments, throwing them out to the flock which waited just outside the cage doors. After the girl did so, the old gobbler picked up her ragged garment in his beak, shook it, and threw back into the cage a beautiful white cotton gown, covered with intricate colored embroidery. As Turkey Girl emerged from the cage in her costume, other turkeys shook her other rags, returning to her soft slippers and other lovely items to wear. Lastly, they gathered about her, brushing her gently with their wings until her hair shone, long and silky, and her entire body was clean and fragrant. She turned and looked at her image in the turkey's watering trough and was completely amazed at the transformation.

The old gobbler once again stepped to the front of the flock with a final admonition to the girl, "Enjoy yourself, certainly, but do not stay until dark or forget that we are your only friends."

Turkey Girl thanked the turkeys, vowed she would never forget them, and then darted down the pathway to join the festivities. When she appeared at the edge of the gaiety, she heard ripples of admiration and puzzlement as the Zunis wondered about the identity of the lovely, wealthy maiden. She did not stand at the edge of the party for long. Soon young men were chatting with her and bringing delicious morsels for her to eat. Never had the girl so enjoyed herself! But alas, as she tossed her hair and danced, she forgot the turkey's warning to return before dark.

"I deserve to eat more food and to dance more, not to run back to a flock of old turkeys," she told herself self-righteously.

At long last the musicians stilled their instruments and the villagers started to return to their homes. Turkey Girl, realizing the lateness of the hour, dashed away from the crowd and raced up the pathway to the turkeys' cages.

Meanwhile the turkeys had grown discontented with the girl's long absence, grumbling that she had either forgotten them or grown ashamed of them.

Finally the old gobbler declared, "Turkey Girl was not as fine as we had thought. Let us flee these cages and live in freedom in one of the canyons."

With that the turkeys flocked out of the cages and disappeared into a nearby canyon filled with scrub oak and other thick brush.

Shortly thereafter, Turkey Girl arrived breathless at the empty cages. Distraught, the girl called to her turkeys and tried to find them in the darkness, but all was lost. Suddenly she looked down to discover that she was once again clad in her filthy rags, a poor Turkey Girl who now did not even have her turkeys to herd.

# Ashpet (United States—Appalachia)

ne time there was a woman with two daughters and a hired gal. They were mean to the hired gal, made her do all the heavy work and wouldn't give her nothin' much to wear. She slept next to the fireplace to keep warm in her skimpy dress and got ashes all over herself. So they called her Ashpet.

Once they were fixin' to go to the church meetin', but a' course, they wouldn't let Ashpet go with them. They told her it was 'cause her looks would shame them, but the truth be known, it was 'cause Ashpet was far purtier than the woman's own two gals.

Well, here they were, gettin' ready for church meetin' and their fire went out, so the woman sent her oldest gal through the gap in the mountains to a witch woman's cabin to get some hot coals. This gal thought she was a might too good to speak with the witch woman, so she just stuck her hand through a big crack in the side of the cabin.

"I come to borry some coals," said the oldest gal, real high falutin' like.

"Come on in and comb my hair, and I'll give ya some," answered the old woman.

"Not on yer life," said the oldest gal.

"Then ya'll not get any of my coals," said the old woman.

So that gal went on back home and the woman sent her next gal through the gap to get some hot coals.

"I come to borry some coals," hollered out the next gal, just as haughty as her sister.

"Come on in and comb my hair, and I'll give ya some," answered the old woman.

"Not on yer life," said the next gal.

"Then ya'll not get any of my coals," said the old woman.

So that gal went on back home and the woman sent Ashpet through the gap to get some hot coals.

"Mornin', ma'am," said Ashpet, real friendly.

"Mornin', Ashpet," replied the old witch woman.

"Ma'am, I come to borry some hot coals, please," said Ashpet.

"Well, come on in and comb my hair purty and you can have all the coals ya want," said the old woman.

"Why, sure," answered Ashpet and skipped on into the cabin to do for the old woman.

As the old witch woman put the live coals into a dried toadstool for Ashpet to carry home, she asked her if she was fixin' to go to church meetin' with the rest of them.

"Lordy, no," declared Ashpet, "by the time I get all the chores done, that church meetin' will be plumb over."

So Ashpet thanked the old woman, hurried on home to build up the fire and fix breakfast, and then started in on all the chores after the others had gone.

Ashpet had scarcely begun when she saw the old witch woman meandering up the path. The gal welcomed the old woman on in, and then watched as the witch woman waved her hobble stick over a mouse as it ran out the front door and turned into as fine a little brown mare as was seen in those parts.

"Now, Ashpet, you sit in this rocker and close your eyes and think of a dress as purty as can be," said the old witch woman.

So Ashpet sat down and thought about a dress, all red and shiny, and fancy shoes to match. The old witch woman waved her hobble stick in front of the gal and when she opened her eyes, there was the very clothes she had been thinkin' of.

While Ashpet washed up, fixin' to go to the church meetin', the old witch woman told her, "As soon as the meetin' commences to break up, you hightail it on back here and hide these fancy things."

When Ashpet went in and sat down at the church meetin', ever'body wondered who she was, not seeing a gal like that in those parts before. Now a rich man's boy was there, and he had his eye on Ashpet. As soon as she hightailed it out of the meetin', he followed her.

Ashpet paid him no mind, but he followed her for a piece, talkin' and all. Finally, when the boy was not lookin', Ashpet eased off one of her shoes and pitched it into the brush.

Then she said all worried like, "Oh my, I've lost one of my shoes somewhere between here and the church. Could you go fetch it for me, please?"

"Why sure I will, li'l gal," said the rich man's boy. "You just wait right here for me."

He soon found the shoe in the brush by the roadside and raced back to where he had left the gal, but there was no one there. Ashpet had hurried on home, leaving the mare in the woods and hiding the dress and shoe.

Well, the rich man's boy was confounded and decided to go from one hollow to the next to find the owner of that shoe. Eventually, he came to the hollow where the woman and her two daughters lived. He walked up on the front porch and told the women that the shoe in his hand had come off the purtiest gal in ten counties, and as soon as he found the owner, he would marry her.

The oldest sister snatched that shoe out of his hand and went in the cabin to try it on, and when it was way too small, she took a butcher knife and cut off part of her toe to fit into that shoe. The she came back out on the porch.

The boy grew suspicious when he looked down and saw her bare foot was as big as a barn, and then when blood started comin' out the top of the shoe, why, he took the shoe right back.

"Let me try," said the next gal, and she took the shoe and went back in the cabin. When her big foot wouldn't fit, she took down the butcher knife and cut off part of her heel, and then came back out on the porch.

Again the boy was suspicious when he saw how terrible big her foot was, and then when he saw blood comin' out the back of the shoe, he took the shoe, spun around, and headed quickly back down the path.

Then he heard a muffled voice comin' from under a big washtub, "Let me try."

When the boy lifted up the corner of the tub, he saw poor Ashpet.

"Why ever are you under here, gal?" he asked.

"'Cause I'm too raggedy and dirty to be with folks," answered Ashpet.

"Well, come on out and try on this shoe," said the boy.

So Ashpet tried on the shoe, and it fit perfectly. She had the rich man's boy wait on the porch while she washed up and put on the other shoe and the dress.

When she came out of the cabin, that boy was mighty pleased. She called her mare from the woods and the two of them rode off to be married, and Ashpet never came back to that hollow again.

# Catskins (United States—Appalachia)

 here once was an orphan gal who stayed on with some folks for her keep. They were mean, never givin' the little gal a dime or decent clothes or nothin'. She had one dress to her name and when it got raggedy, she took to patchin' it with old cat hides to where, finally, the dress was most all cat hides. So folks called the gal Catskins.

One day the wife up and died, and it wasn't too long before the man was wantin' Catskins for a bride.

"I will be yer wife," said Catskins, "if first you fetch me a dress with the colors of all the fish in the sea."

But as soon as the man got her that dress, Catskins said, "I will be yer wife if you fetch me a dress with the colors of all the flowers in the meadow."

The man did, but by now he was a mite perturbed and wanted to have the weddin' real soon.

"If I could just have your flyin' box, then I reckon I'd be all ready," said Catskins.

Well, the man did not want to part ways with his flyin' box, but on the other hand, he sure did want Catskins for a wife, so he finally gave it over to her.

Catskins went into the back room to put on one of the dresses for her weddin', but instead, she bundled up those dresses, put them in the flyin' box, and took off through the window for a rich man's house some ways away.

When she got there, she hid the flyin' box with the fine dresses under a rock, and then went up to the house to ask for work. They gave her a job, but just in the kitchen for she was a sight for sore eyes.

By and by all the folks round about were a fixin' to go to a big barn dance at the home of the richest man in ten counties. His son was of a marrying age, so all the gals around were hoping they could catch his eye.

The woman where Catskins worked said, "You can go if you've a mind to and look through the winda's with the other po' folk."

Catskins allowed as she would think it over. But soon as they all left, she raced to that rock and touched it. Fast as greased lightnin', the flyin' box came up and opened, and Catskins took out the dress that had the colors of all the fish in the sea, put it on, and then flew with the box to the barn dance.

When Catskins walked into that barn, folks were amazed. They didn't know one gal in those parts who looked like that.

Now the rich man's son danced several squares with her and wanted to make her acquaintance, but out the door she went before he had a chance.

When the family got home, they found Catskins sittin' by the fire in her old catskin dress.

"Did you go and have a look-see through the winda's at the dance?" asked the woman.

"Yes, ma'am, I did," answered Catskins.

"Then you must have seen that real purty gal there," said the woman. "No one knows who she is, but the rich folks are fixin' to have another dance tomorra' night just so the son can see that gal again."

With that everyone went to bed so they could rest up for the next night's dance.

The next night went about the same, only Catskins wore the dress with the colors of all the flowers in the meadow.

This time the rich man's son kept a tight hold on the purty gal's hand, and round about midnight, he slipped a ring on her finger. But like before, the gal slipped away with nary a trace.

Catskins flew home and hid the ring in with her dresses in the flyin' box. The rich man's son was stuck on that gal, but he couldn't find hide nor hair of her.

Finally he commenced to get sick. Gals round about started bakin' sweets and all, thinkin' maybe he would like them and their cookin' and forget about the purty gal from the dances.

Catskins got the idea to make a nice cake for the boy and slipped the ring into it just before she put on the icing. But when the cake was ready, the woman said *she* would take it up to the fine house, bein's Catskins was such a sight and all.

So the old woman traipsed on up to the fancy house, thinkin' highly of herself with the fine cake to give.

When the boy's mama cut a piece for him, the ring fell out.

"Who baked this cake?" hollered the boy, as he purt near leaped out of bed.

"Why, I did," said the woman.

"That cain't be the Lord's truth," returned the boy angrily. "You fetch who ever baked this cake here on the double!"

The woman went back for Catskins, who had already figured out what happened and allowed she would go there herself.

She first went back to the flyin' box under the rock and took out the dress with the colors of all the flowers in the meadow and then flew to the rich man's house.

Catskins stood there in the doorway, and when the rich man's boy saw her, he grinned from ear to ear, "You are the one," said he. "Will you marry me?"

They married and lived good.

# Cam and the Magic Fish (Vietnam)

There once was a man who had two daughters. The older daughter, named Tam, was sour natured and homely and deeply jealous of her younger sister, Cam. Cam, on the other hand, was as sweet and happy as she was pretty.

One day their father decided he would enjoy fish for dinner, so he asked the daughters to go fishing.

"I will give a beautiful jade necklace to the daughter who can catch the most fish," promised the father.

So the maidens took their buckets and nets and hurried to the village pond. Cam quickly caught many fish, arousing jealousy in her sister Tam.

"See the lovely white lotus blossoms on the other side of the pond," Tam pointed out to her sister. "Why don't you go over there and pluck a bouquet of those flowers for father's dinner table?"

Cam agreed with her older sister. Since she already had a bucket full of fish, she waded over to pick the pretty flowers.

When Cam returned, however, she discovered that Tam was gone and so were Cam's fish. Upset by her sister's treachery, Cam burst into tears.

A genie suddenly appeared at Cam's side, "Don't weep, fair maiden. Soon all will be well for you. There is left a tiny blue fish in your bucket. Take it home and tend it well."

With that, the genie vanished. Cam looked into the bucket and, true to the genie's words, there swam a tiny blue fish.

After eating their fish dinner that evening, the father awarded the beautiful jade necklace to Tam. Cam contented herself with the little fish, which she placed in a bowl, and said nothing to her sister. This seemed to make Tam more angry rather than satisfying her. Eventually her jealous grew so poisonous that she took Cam's little blue fish and killed it, burying it beneath a palm tree in their courtyard. When Cam discovered that Tam had killed her fish, she ran to her room in tears.

Again, a genie appeared at her side, "Don't weep, fair maiden. Soon all will be well for you. I will show you where the bones of your little blue fish are buried. Dig them up and rebury them under your bed. After a hundred days, take them back out."

The genie floated over the spot under the palm tree where the fish was buried and then instantly disappeared. Cam immediately did as she was told, digging up the fish's bones, wrapping them in silk, and reverently placing them under her bed. She carefully kept track of the days. When one hundred days had passed, she took out the silk packet with the bones from under her bed. As she opened it, her dark eyes grew wide in astonishment. The bones had turned into a pair of beautiful slippers, encrusted with precious jewels and decorated with gold and silver.

The entire village was amazed at the exquisite beauty of the slippers. Cam generously loaned them to other girls to wear, but, alas, they would fit none but Cam.

Then one morning while Cam was working in her father's rice paddies, a big black crow flew overhead, attracted by the glittering jewels of the slippers near the water's edge. Suddenly, without warning the crow swooped down, snatched one of the slippers, and flew off. Cam was very upset at the loss of the lovely slipper, though she remembered the genie's promise that all would be well and so went about her work as before.

Meanwhile, the crow became overwhelmed with the weight of the jewel encrusted slipper in its beak and dropped it. It so happened that it fell into one of the royal gardens of the king.

A couple of days later while the king's son was wandering through the fragrant gardens, he happened upon the exquisite slipper. The shoe was so tiny and unique and, obviously, so valuable that the king's son thought the owner would make a perfect bride.

The king sent messengers with the jeweled slipper for young maidens throughout the kingdom to try on. It would fit none of their feet, causing the king's son to become very discouraged.

At last the messengers came to the village of Cam and Tam. When young maidens began trying on the slipper, they recognized it as being Cam's and sent for her. Tam pushed ahead of her sister in her haste to try on the slipper, but this time no amount of trickery would work. The slipper did not fit Tam, but perfectly fit the dainty foot of the lovely Cam. The messengers were instructed to immediately bring the maiden whose foot fit the slipper back to the royal palace for the wedding.

The pair was married in a magnificent royal wedding ceremony and all was well, just as the genie had promised.

# Discussion Questions

### Prereading Focus Question

- As you listen, think of the differences and similarities among the tales. What was the obstacle that each girl had to overcome?

### Reading Focus Question

- Though conditions seemed impossible for the main characters in each of these folktales, they never gave up. Perhaps this theme of hope is what has made these folktales so enduring and so popular. Though the folktales presented here on the theme of "Never Give Up" have only girls as the main characters, there are some folktales with this theme that have boys as the main characters. There are not nearly as many, and they are not nearly as popular as the ones with girls. Why do you think this is the case?

### Post-Reading Questions

- (Return to Focus Question) What was each girl's obstacle?

- After hearing the tales that contain a magic fish from Vietnam and China (Yeh-Shen), it would be logical to expect a magic fish in the tale from Korea. What magic animals are in the Korean story? Which tales include magic serpents or snakes? Are those cultures close to one another?

- Do any of these tales have slippers like the folktales from Europe? Are the cultures which have slippers in their folktales close together geographically?

- Listen to the story of Rhodopis in "The Egyptian Cinderella" (see Bibliography, page 167) and "Cam and the Magic Fish" (on pages 151–153). What important feature do these two tales have in common?

- Listen to "Princess Furball" by Charlotte Huck (see Bibliography, page 168) as well as "Ashpet" (pages 147–149) and "The Princess and the Sea Serpent" (pages 130–132). What important feature do these the tales have in common?

- Only two tales mention a time factor for returning from the dance. Which ones have this feature? (One is not included in this unit.)

- Why would stories from cultures located so far apart have similar elements? (No one knows an exact answer to this.)

The Brazilian and the Algonquin folktales both have *pourquoi* elements. What are they?

Which folktale does not actually fit the theme? Are the two Native American folktales similar?

What characteristics tie these folktales together?

Why do you think it might be difficult to trace the origins of these stories?

# Never Give Up Map

*Directions:* Find the continent for each folktale. Choose a colored pencil or fine-tipped marker to color both the continent and the matching box in the legend. If you study more variants than there are different colors in your pencil assortment, you can create stripes, dots, and other patterns.

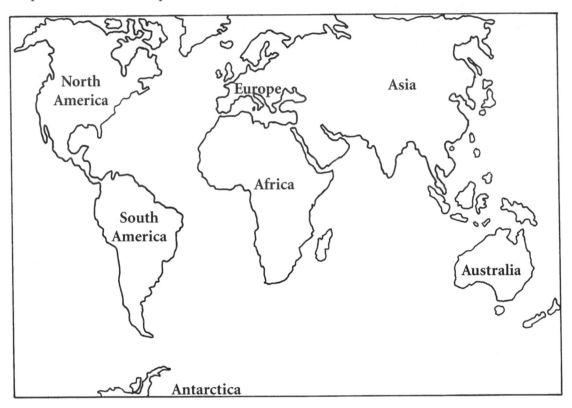

☐ Africa-Lesotho ("Polo, the Snake-Girl")

☐ Brazil ("The Princess and the Sea Serpent")

☐ Ireland ("Trembling")

☐ Italy ("Cenerentola")

☐ Korea ("Kongjee")

☐ Norway ("Kari Woodendress")

☐ United States–Algonquin Indian ("Little Burnt Face")

☐ United States–Zuni Indian ("Turkey Girl")

☐ United States–Appalachian ("Ashpet" and "Catskins")

☐ Vietnam ("Cam and the Magic Fish")

# Comparative Checklist

*Directions:* After hearing several variants, it is easy to confuse elements from them. Fill out this checklist as you hear each one and then it will be easy to remember the important parts.

**Name of girl (main character):**

_____

**Family situation (minor characters):**

❏ stepsister(s)
❏ sister(s)
❏ stepmother
❏ mother
❏ father
❏ special young man _____

_____

**Special animals (minor characters):**

❏ snake or serpent
❏ fish
❏ other_____

**Important clothing (setting):**

❏ shoe _____
❏ ring
❏ dress(es) _____

_____

❏ other_____

**Special effects (plot):**

❏ gore/violence _____

_____

❏ magic _____

_____

**"Threeness" (plot):**

❏ same event occurs three times _____

_____

❏ three similar items _____

_____

**Ending (plot):**

❏ married with children: #_____

❏ revenge for stepsisters/stepmother

_____

❏ forgiveness for stepsisters/ stepmother _____

_____

❏ lived happily ever after

# Trivia Game

*Directions:* Write in the culture of a variant. Next write an interesting question about a character, event, or element from that story. Write the answer. Keep your cards for a Trivia Game at the end of the unit.

**Cinderella Trivia**

Culture: *Irish*
Question: *Who gave Trembling beautiful clothing so she could attend church?*

Answer: *An old hen woman.*

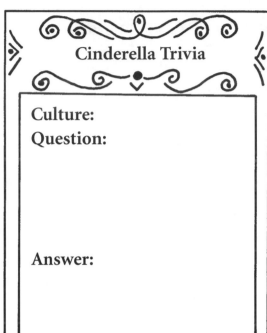

**Cinderella Trivia**

Culture:
Question:

Answer:

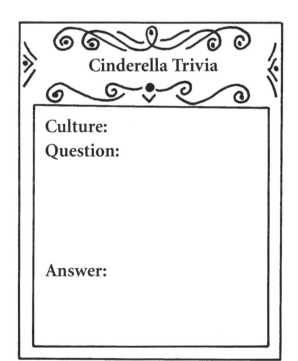

**Cinderella Trivia**

Culture:
Question:

Answer:

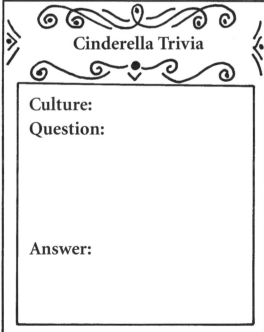

**Cinderella Trivia**

Culture:
Question:

Answer:

# Academy Awards

*Directions:* Each variant makes a different, though distinct, impression on the listener. In your opinion, which one deserves each of the Academy Awards below. Write them in pencil until you have heard them all in case you change your mind. You may choose the last award category.

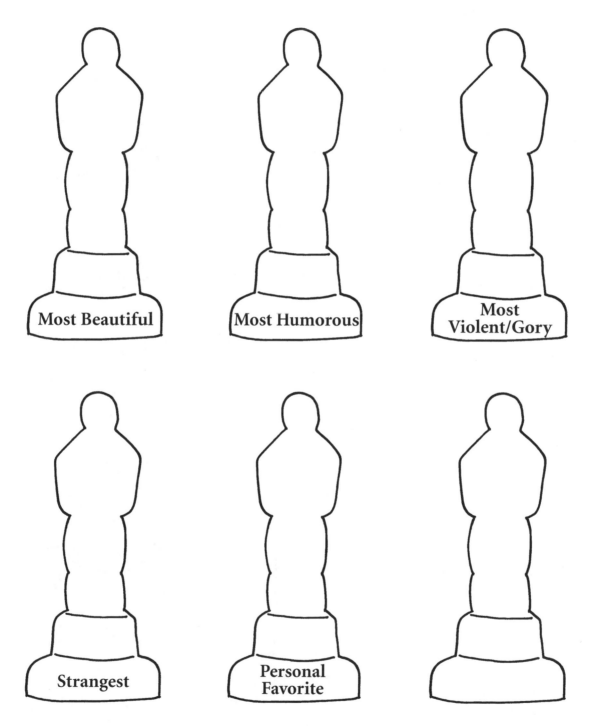

**Most Beautiful**

**Most Humorous**

**Most Violent/Gory**

**Strangest**

**Personal Favorite**

# Cinderella Variant Pop-Up

*Directions:* Research the costumes and background of a favorite culture's "Cinderella" character. Decorate your character with markers, fabric, and yarn. Mount the character on a 12" × 17" sheet of paper according to the diagram below. Write the name of the culture on the top half of the paper. These can be displayed on counter tops or stapled to a wall display.

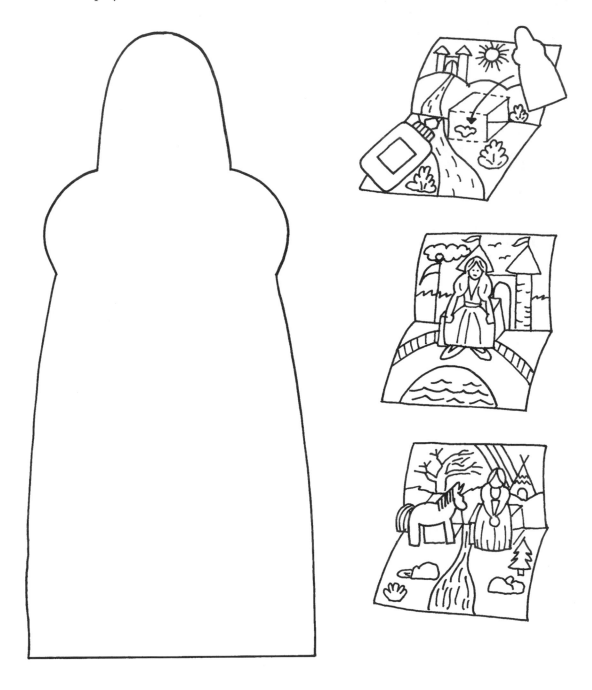

# Folklore Stereotypes

*Directions:* Read or listen to the clues on the following page that describe stereotypical characters or concepts in the French "Cinderella." Each word(s) will fit on the chart below. Then answer the questions at the bottom of the page.

_____**C**_____

_____**I**_____

_____**N**_____

_____**D**_____

_____**E**_____

_____**R**_____

_____**E**_____

_____**L**_____

_____**L**_____

_____**A**_____

**Are any of these stereotypes accurate?**




**How could belief in any of them be misleading or even harmful to people today?**

continued

# Folklore Stereotype Puzzle Clues

**C**  No average man is good enough for a husband, only a royal son, often called a
_____.

**I**  Most Cinderella stories end with the main characters living this way ever after.

**N**  Cinderella is never a senior citizen; in fact, she is always _____.

**D**  Cinderella always has to _____ _____ in the first part of the story before she can enjoy a life of leisure in the end.

**E**  This stereotypical character is always wicked and jealous of her new husband's daughter.

**R**  This is the greatest prize for Cinderella; it is a long word, but not a person.

**E**  They are ugly, as well as mean.

**L**  Cinderella is no "plain Jane"; she is always _____. (Two different words could work here.)

**L**  Prince Charming is never poor; he and his family have great
_____.

**A**  At the end of her leg, Cinderella always has a _____
_____.

*Answers to Folklore Stereotype Puzzle: prince, happily, young, work hard, stepmother, marriage, stepsisters, beautiful or lovely, wealth, small foot*

## Lost Ending

*Directions:* The ending of your favorite variant was accidentally torn away. Use your imagination to write a new ending. The final words on the piece of torn paper gives you a start on your own creative ending!

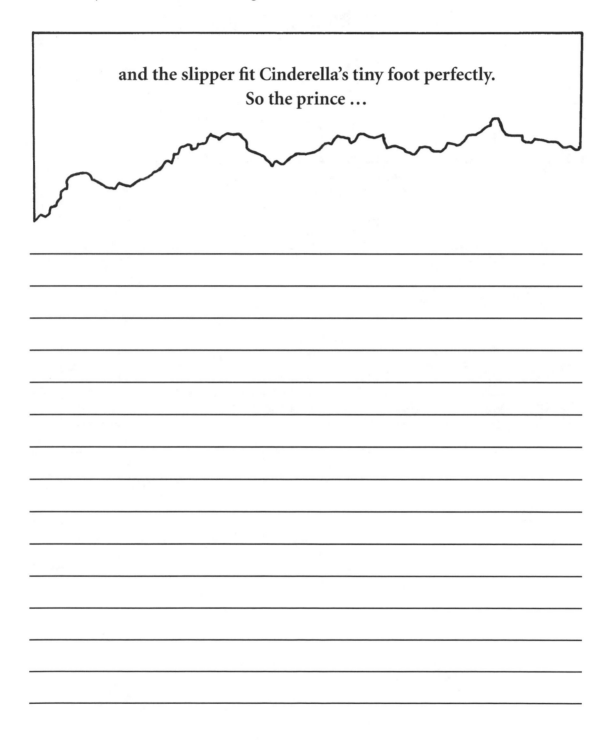

**and the slipper fit Cinderella's tiny foot perfectly.
So the prince ...**

_____

_____

_____

_____

_____

_____

_____

_____

_____

_____

_____

_____

_____

# Cinderella Crossword

continued

# Cinderella Crossword Clues

## Across

3  the name of the maiden in the other Appalachian variant

6  the name of the youngest daughter in the Irish variant

8  the most widely spread folktale of all time

9  the Great Wind pulled this across the sky

10  the magic animal in the Norwegian variant

11  the name of the Italian Cinderella

13  the magic animal that helped Kongjee fill the water jar in the Korean variant

17  the wicked creature in the Norwegian variant

18  the magic character in the Irish variant

19  in the Algonquin tale these leaves always quake when the Great Wind comes near

20  the magic animal in Cenerentola

21  the Prince of Ireland fought this long for the hand of the maiden

## Down

1  the last name of the girl in the Norwegian variant

2  the name of the Indian tibe in "Turkey Girl"

3  first precious metal in Norwegian variant

4  the older sister in the Vietnamese variant

5  the animal in the Brazilian variant

7  the magic character in the Vietnamese variant

9  the type of shoe that Kongjee lost in the Korean variant

10  the type of knife used in the Appalachian variant

12  the name of the maiden in the Appalachian variant with six letters

13  the animals in the Zuni variant

14  the name of the African Cinderella

15  the African Cinderella hid under this snake skin

16  a dress made of the colors of all the flowers in the _____

Name ______________________________

# Cinderella Crossword Answers

| | | | | | | | | | | | | | | | | | | |
|---|---|---|---|---|---|---|---|---|---|---|---|---|---|---|---|---|---|---|
| | | 1 W | | | | | | | | | | | | | | | | |
| | | O | | | | 2 Z | | | | | | | | | | | | |
| | | O | | | | U | | | | 3 C | A | 4 T | S | K | I | N | 5 S | |
| | | D | | | | N | | | | O | | A | | | | | E | |
| 6 T | R | E | M | B | L | I | N | 7 G | | P | | M | | | | | R | |
| | | N | | | | | | E | | P | | | | | | | P | |
| | | D | | | | 8 C | I | N | D | E | R | E | L | L | A | | E | |
| | | R | | | | | | I | | R | | | | | | | N | |
| | | E | | | | 9 S | L | E | D | | 10 B | U | L | L | | | T | |
| | | S | | | | A | | | | | U | | | | | | | |
| | | S | | 11 C | E | N | E | R | E | N | T | O | L | 12 A | | | | |
| | | | | | | D | | | | | C | | | S | | | | |
| | | | | 13 T | O | A | D | | | | H | | | H | | | | |
| | | | | U | | L | | | | | E | | | P | | | | 14 P |
| | | | | R | | | | | | | R | | | E | | 15 B | | O |
| | | | | K | | | | | 16 M | | | | | 17 T | R | O | L | L |
| | | | 18 H | E | N | W | I | F | E | | | | | | | A | | O |
| | | | | Y | | | | | A | | | | | | | | | |
| | | | 19 A | S | P | E | N | | 20 D | O | V | E | | | | | | |
| | | | | | | | | | O | | | | | | | | | |
| | | | | | | | | | 21 W | E | E | K | | | | | | |

# Bibliography

There have been several outstanding picture books of Cinderella variants published in recent years by noted children's authors and illustrators. They include variants from all over the world. These superb books add an appealing visual element to this literary unit.

Climo, Shirley. *The Egyptian Cinderella*. New York: HarperCollins, 1989.

Created by Shirley Climo and Ruth Heller (illustrator), the origin of this Egyptian variant dates back to the first century B.C. Careful attention to detail in the gorgeous illustrations, along with the well-told tale, make this a basic book in a folktale collection. Available in both hardcover and paperback.

———. *The Korean Cinderella*. New York: HarperCollins, 1993.

Climo and Heller are back—this time with a book even more rich and colorful than their Egyptian variant.

Coburn, Jewell Coburn, and Tzexa Cherta Lee. *Jouanah: A Hmong Cinderella*. Arcadia, Calif.: Shen's Books, 1996.

This large, beautifully illustrated and designed picture book tells the tale of a poor Hmong girl who is cruelly mistreated by her stepmother, but eventually triumphs with the help of her dead mother's spirit.

Cohlene, Terri. *Little Firefly*. Mahwah, N.J.: Watermill Press, 1990.

Available in paperback, this colorful version of the the Algonquin tale of "Little Burnt Face" is high quality. It also contains a section telling the history and customs of the Algonquin people.

Compton, Joanne. *Ashpet: An Appalachian Tale*. New York: Holiday House, 1994.

This delightful variant is told and illustrated by the husband and wife team with great humor. Sure to tickle audiences.

De Regniers, Beatrice Schenk. *Little Sister and the Month Brothers*. New York: Seabury Press, 1976.

Still in print, this fine production by illustrator Margot Tomes and folklore specialist Beatrice Schenk deRegniers tells the Slavic variant of "Cinderella." The distinguishing feature is the intervention of the Month Brothers, magical characters who bring the weather for each of the twelve months and save Little Sister.

Greaves, Margaret. *Tattercoats*. New York: Clarkson N. Potter, 1990.

Margaret Chamberlain uses watercolor and pen-and-ink for the lively illustrations of the English folktale "Tattercoats." The retelling, which is less harsh than the original tale, matches the joyous quality of the illustrations.

Han, Oki S., and Stephanie Haboush Plunkett. *Kongi and Potgi: A Cinderella Story from Korea*. New York: Dial Books for Young Readers, 1996.

Han and Plunkett have created a outstandingly illustrated Korean variant.

Hogrogian, Nonny. *Cinderella*. New York: Greenwillow, 1981.

Hogrogian used the German Ash Maiden variant for her retelling. The illustrations are done in soft watercolors to match the text, which has been softened somewhat from the original.

Hooks, William H. *Moss Gown*. New York: Clarion, 1987.

This old American tale of the deep South combines the "Cinderella" theme as well as part of the European folktale "Meat Loves Salt." Well-known illustrator Donald Carrick does a superb job of depicting the fine mansions and moss-hanging trees of the old South.

Huck, Charlotte. *Princess Furball*. New York: Greenwillow, 1989.

Two outstanding talents in children's publishing teamed efforts to create this version of the German tale "Allerleirauh" (translated varyingly as "Many Furred Creature" or "Many Furs"). This book features an energetic retelling and vivid illustrations.

Jacobs, Joseph. *Tattercoats*. New York: Putnam, 1989.

Margot Tomes has beautifully illustrated the original English variant. Her careful research of period clothing, housing, and landscape is quite apparent.

Louie, Ai-Ling. *Yeh-Shen*. New York: Philomel, 1982.

Perhaps the crown jewel of the picture-book variants is *Yeh-Shen*, lyrically retold and creatively illustrated by Ed Young.

Lum, Darrell. *The Golden Slipper: A Vietnamese Legend*. Mahwah, N.J.: Troll Associates, 1994.

The Troll paperback publication is a brightly illustrated watercolor version of the Vietnamese tale of Tam and Cam. Part of the "Legends of the World" series, this story has more magical animals than the other versions and is easier for children to read.

Marshak, Samuel. *The Month Brothers.* New York: William Morrow, 1983.

This Czechoslovakian variant has been illustrated in lovely detail by Diane Stanley. The colorful, full-page paintings and engrossing story make this an excellent choice for large-group story time.

Martin, Rafe. *The Rough-Face Girl.* New York: Putnam, 1992.

David Shannon has painted beautiful pictures for this Algonquin Indian tale from the Great Lakes region.

Mehta, Lila. *The Enchanted Anklet: A Cinderella Story from India.* Ontario, Canada: Lilmur Publishing, 1985.

In this thousand-year-old tale from India, a magic snake with a jewel in its head delivers the poor stepdaughter from her life of misery to an enchanted ending with marriage to a prince. Many of the Indian terms are explained in a glossary at the end. An anklet serves the purpose of the slipper in this interesting, though amateurishly illustrated, variant.

Pollock, Penny. *The Turkey Girl: A Zuni Cinderella Story.* Boston: Little, Brown, 1996.

Ed Young used oil crayons to fill the large pages with gorgeous color and soft images. The graceful retelling blends perfectly with the art.

San Souci, Robert D. *Sootface: An Ojibwa Cinderella Story.* New York: A Doubleday Book for Young Readers, 1994.

The San Souci brothers, Robert and Daniel, have created a moving and beautifully illustrated rendition of the beloved Indian tale from the Great Lakes region.

———. *The Talking Eggs.* New York: Dial Books for Young Readers, 1989.

Robert San Souci and Jerry Pinkney have teamed to create this outstanding Caldecott Honor book. While the "Cinderella" connection is not as clear in this story as others, it still has many parallels.

Schroeder, Alan. *Smoky Mountain Rose: An Appalachian Cinderella.* New York: Dial Books for Young Readers, 1997.

Told in a broad dialect, this rollicking "Cinderella" tale is a retold variant of "Catskins" and "Ashpet." Brad Sneed's robust watercolors add to the hilarity of this outstanding picture book.

Schroeder, Alan. *Lily and the Wooden Bowl*. New York: Doubleday Books for Young Readers, 1994.

Yoriko Ito painted the exquisite illustrations for this fascinating tale from Japan. A dying grandmother places a large lacquer bowl on the head of her granddaughter with the admonition to never remove it. After many trials and difficulties, Lily marries the wealthy landowner's kind son in a surprising ending.

Sherman, Josepha. *Rachel the Clever and Other Jewish Folktales*. Little Rock, Ark.: August House, 1993.

The chapter entitled "Cinderella" is a marvelous variant from Poland that contains the "meat loves salt" motif. This fine tale, with the lesson to look beyond the clothes to the person, should be illustrated as a single volume for greater exposure to large numbers of children.

Steptoe, John. *Mufaro's Beautiful Daughters*. New York: Lothrop, Lee & Shepard, 1987.

This beautifully told and illustrated African tale is a Caldecott Honor book.

Vuong, Luong Dyer. *The Brocaded Slipper and Other Vietnamese Tales*. Reading, Mass.: Addison-Wesley, 1982.

The "Cinderella" tale featured here, among other Vietnamese folktales, is much longer and more complex than the rewritten version found in the "Never Give Up" unit.

Wilson, Barbar Ker. *Wishbones*. New York: Bradbury Press, 1993.

This Chinese story of Yeh Hsien is nicely illustrated. The author noted that "the story of Cinderella is now 'modern' once again." This is certainly proven by the quality and quantity of books listed in this bibliography.

Winthrop, Elizabeth. *Vasilissa the Beautiful*. New York: HarperCollins, 1991.

This Russian variant has been recently published in America with rich, colorful illustrations by Alexander Koshkin in a format faithful to the old Russian culture.

### French Cinderella Versions

Brown, Marcia. *Cinderella*. New York: Charles Scribners', 1954.

This is the famous version which won the 1955 Caldecott Award. Illustrated with woodcuts, the book is still in print, including paperback editions.

Delamare, David. *Cinderella*. New York: Simon & Schuster, 1993.

> Beautifully illustrated within a setting of Venice's canals and gondolas, this version is quite appealing and lends itself to comparative study with other colorful renditions.

Ehrlich, Amy. *Cinderella*. New York: Dial Books, 1985.

> Susan Jeffers has illustrated this large, lovely book with her characteristic double-page lush spreads. This book brought renewed interest in "Cinderella" since an outstanding version had not been produced for several years prior to 1985.

Elwell, Peter. *Cinderella*. Chicago: Contemporary Books, 1988.

> Jada Rowland's soft, evocative watercolor paintings are the outstanding feature of this version. Elwell tries to make logical explanations for the events in the story, forgetting that magic and logic do not often combine well.

French, Fiona. *Cinderella*. New York: Oxford University Press, 1987.

> Though painted with brilliant watercolors and filled with details of French clothing and hairstyles, this version has an abbreviated text which makes it more suitable for younger audiences.

Galdone, Paul. *Cinderella*. New York: McGraw-Hill, 1978.

> Galdone's smooth retelling and lively, detailed illustrations make this older version a perennial favorite. His comical drawings of the stepsisters give the impression of humor more than evil.

Goode, Diane. *Cinderella*. New York: Alfred A. Knopf, 1988.

> This recent edition is well done. The pictures of the mice turning into horses and the lizards into footmen are especially creative.

Hague, Michael. *Cinderella and Other Tales from Perrault*. New York: Henry Holt, 1989.

> Michael Hague has illustrated Perrault's original collection of eight fairy tales.

Innocenti, Roberto. *Cinderella*. Mankato, Minn.: Creative Education, 1983.

> This is the most unusual of all the "Cinderella" books in print. While the text remains faithful to Perrault, the illustrations are set in the 1920s. This one would be excellent for comparison.

Karlin, Barbara. *Cinderella*. Boston: Little, Brown, 1989.

> James Marshall's hilarious illustrations and Karlin's lively retelling take this book close to parody. A rollicking good time!

Perrault, Charles. *Cinderella* or *The Little Glass Slipper*. New York: Bradbury Press, 1972.

> Though currently out of print in hardcover, Errol Le Cain's rendition has been reprinted in paperback by Puffin Books. His trademark use of colorful borders, exquisite detail, and exciting retellings combine to create a magical version.

*Walt Disney Cinderella*. New York: Gallery Books, 1986.

> The Disney version is still available and is worthwhile to compare to other versions.

### Parodies

Brooke, William. *The Telling of the Tales*. New York: Harper & Row, 1990.

> This clever parody deals with the wisdom of choosing a wife on the basis of a shoe. Well written and engaging, "The Fitting of the Slipper" is an excellent springboard for discussion or creative writing.

Cole, Babette. *Prince Cinders*. New York: G. P. Putnam's, 1987.

> Cole's book, filled with exuberant, colorful pictures, is a hilarious romp and a marvelous example of humorous parody.

Dahl, Roald. *Revolting Rhymes*. New York: Bantam Books, 1986.

> This poem "Cinderella," told in rhyming couplets, fits in well with humorous parodies and is highly appealing. It is written in Dahl's highly irreverent, madcap style and should be read carefully before sharing with children.

Jackson, Ellen. *Cinder Edna*. New York: Lothrop, Lee & Shepard, 1994.

> This refreshing parody features two girls: a boring Cinderella who ends up with the vain prince and Cinder Edna, a spunky, plain-looking girl who ends up with the prince's more interesting younger brother, Rupert. Lively, colorful illustrations by Kevin O'Malley add to the fun.

Lattimore, Deborah Nourse. *Cinderhazel: The Cinderella Of Halloween*. New York: The Blue Sky Press, 1997.

> Younger children will roar at this hilarious parody. Cinderhazel is a witch who *loves* dirt. Her fairy godwitch turns Cinderhazel's broom into a magic vacuum

cleaner to ride to the ball where the prince turns out to be, yes, a dirtball! Riotous pictures complement this laughfest.

Levine, Gail Carson. *Ella Enchanted*. New York: HarperCollins, 1997.

This delightful novel aimed at girls in upper elementary and middle school mixes fairytale elements of magical kingdoms, powers, and characters with the "Cinderella" story. The main character is a teenage girl who lives a parody of the original tale, but with many intriguing twists and turns. The use of a made-up language makes this book difficult to read aloud, but a highly recommended novel for girls who enjoy medieval-style literature with a strong, young heroine.

Meddaugh, Susan. *Cinderella's Rat*. Boston: Houghton Mifflin, 1997.

This clever picture book keeps the reader guessing all the way to the last page. It begins with sibling rats caught in a cage; the brother rat is changed by a fairy god-mother into a coachboy to take Cinderella to the castle. There he gravitates into the castle kitchen where, at last, he has an abundance to eat. Then his sister (who is still a rat) is caught in the larder and nearly killed. There are several additional surprises in store for the reader before the ending. This book would lend itself to children's predictions throughout the reading.

Myers, Bernice. *Sidney Rella and the Glass Sneaker*. New York: Macmillan, 1985.

While not as lively or as colorfully illustrated as *Prince Cinders*, *Sidney Rella* is a clever and humorous parody. The glass sneaker is an amusing touch.

Perlman, Janet. *Cinderella Penguin or The Little Glass Flipper*. New York: Viking, 1992.

This clever parody done in a large picture-book format is filled with medieval garbed penguins. Sure to delight a youthful audience.

Scieszka, Jonn, and Lane Smith. *The Stinky Cheese Man and Other Fairly Stupid Tales*. New York: Viking Penguin, 1992.

If you are looking for a bizarre parody of folktales, this is it. Winner of a 1992 Caldecott Honor Book Award, this book tickles childrens' funnybones.

Shorto, Russell. *Cinderella/The Untold Story of Cinderella*. New York: Carol Publishing, 1991.

While not an outstanding version of "Cinderella," this book can serve as an interesting model of a parody. The "Upside Down Tale" tells the story from the point of view of Della, the stepsister, and has an interesting twist.

# Index of Folktales

# Index of Activity Pages

372.8   GARRITY, LINDA K.
GAR       THE TALE SPINNER

| | DATE DUE | | |
|---|---|---|---|
| | | | |
| | | | |
| | | | |
| | | | |
| | | | |
| | | | |
| | | | |
| | | | |
| | | | |
| | | | |